Throne
of Profit

Small Business Strategy that Works

William Hassell

© 2025 William Hassell. All rights reserved.
Published by Throne of Profit, LLC
throneofprofit.com

No part of this publication may be reproduced, stored in a retrieval system, or transmitted in any form or by any means—electronic, mechanical, photocopying, recording, or otherwise—without the prior written permission of the publisher, except in the case of brief quotations used in reviews or scholarly works.

For permissions, licensing inquiries, or bulk orders, contact: info@throneofprofit.com

Title: Throne of Profit
Author: William Hassell
Cover Design: William Hassell
Cover Image: Created with the assistance of Adobe Express generative AI tools
Interior Design: William Hassell
Publisher: Throne of Profit, LLC

ISBN: 979-8-9990486-0-8 (Hardcover with Jacket)
ISBN: 979-8-9990486-1-5 (eBook)
ISBN: 979-8-9990486-2-2 (Paperback)
ISBN: 979-8-9990486-3-9 (Case Laminate Hardcover)

Library of Congress Control Number: 2025910977

Printed in the United States of America
First Edition

This is a work of fiction. Names, characters, places, and events are either the product of the author's imagination or used fictitiously. Any resemblance to actual persons, living or dead, or actual events is purely coincidental.

Trademarks and Proprietary Content

Throne of Profit™, Throne of Profit System™, ToP Strategy Model™, ToP Action Model™, and ToP Measurement Model™ are trademarks of Throne of Profit, LLC. These marks refer to proprietary frameworks and business methodologies developed and owned by the author and publisher.

The content, tools, and models presented in this publication are original intellectual property protected under United States copyright law and common-law trademark rights. They may not be copied, adapted, distributed, or incorporated into other works without express written permission or a licensing agreement.

All other trademarks used herein are the property of their respective owners.

Disclaimer

The content in this book and any accompanying materials—including but not limited to the *Throne of Profit System*™, *the ToP Strategy Model*™, *the ToP Action Model*™, *and the ToP Measurement Model*™—is provided for general informational and educational purposes only. Nothing in this publication constitutes professional advice, and no part of the book should be interpreted as a substitute for consultation with qualified financial, legal, tax, or business professionals.

While this system reflects tested methodologies and strategic principles, the author and publisher make no representations, warranties, or guarantees as to any specific business outcomes or financial results. All business ventures carry inherent risks, and outcomes are affected by numerous variables beyond the scope or control of this book.

By reading this book or implementing any aspect of the system, the reader acknowledges full responsibility for their actions and business decisions and agrees to hold harmless the author, publisher, licensors, affiliates, and any related parties from any claims, damages, or losses—financial or otherwise—that may arise.

Use of the *Throne of Profit System*™ and its derivative frameworks does not create any form of advisory, fiduciary, or client relationship with the author or publisher. Any application of the materials is at the reader's sole discretion and risk.

For licensed use, reproduction, or integration into organizational frameworks, written permission and licensing agreements are required. Unauthorized reproduction or distribution is strictly prohibited.

To My Family

PREFACE

I began this book while returning from a client site visit. The idea was born from contemplating how to assist small business owners in bettering their business approach; a way that is smarter and more efficient. My site visit yielded productive results, and I scheduled another meeting for six months later. The sheer number of positive and negative decisions, potentially made before our next encounter, concerned me as I drove off. I was thinking about an outline, advice booklet, spreadsheet, or something that might help between visits. A once-a-month call wouldn't cut it; I needed something more. I then started thinking of books I had read over the years... maybe I could offer some suggestions.

Lots of books that can be found online for download or on shelves in bookstores and airports throughout the nation seem to be written for a particular type of audience; the audience seems to be most typically working for Fortune 500 or 100 level companies, consulting with or servicing those companies, or people that aspire to be in one of those groups. My day-to-day work primarily involves collaborating with business owners who have fewer than 100 employees associated with their company; the average annual revenue for these enterprises is typically under $50 million. The type of owner leading these companies has never been on a corporate jet, doesn't shop in Milan, or ski the Alps. The average owner's desire notwithstanding, they lack the time or motivation to read a list of 20–50 books that could influence their decision-making. An idea suddenly struck me: I could write a short, punchy book. The goal would be to offer a framework for thinking slightly better about decisions for your division or business.

So, find a way that suits you—a chapter or two each day, perhaps, or a Saturday night—and enjoy the read. Most importantly, jot down your ideas. This is an attempt to offer valuable, easily digestible content that inspires you to implement an idea or begin a project. Remember…

Despite any shortcomings, successes, failures, triumphs, challenges, false-starts, or anything else that might describe your previous or current actions and emotions, please take comfort in knowing we are all only human. Regardless of age or position, everyone makes mistakes in life and business. How one handles mistakes determines whether one experiences defeat or victory. Reading this shows you're on the beautiful path of growth and learning. And, if you are on that path, hope exists. Although hope isn't a business plan, it can start self-discovery and development. So… from one businessperson to another, I wish you the most tremendous success.

Contents

PREFACE vii
THE JOURNEY 1
    Stranded at the Airport 3
    Profit by Design Not by Degree 14
    Changing the Lens 21
    The Throne of Profit 31
    When Effort Isn't Enough 42
    Change With the Times 51
    Beyond the Smile 59
    Rewrite the Story 67
    Between Job and Dreams 81
    Always Have a Plan B 95
    Action! 106
    More Than Coffee 116
    Where Food Meets Purpose 123
    Beyond the Bike 129
    A Step Toward the Throne 138
THE NOTEBOOK 149
FINAL CALL — CLAIM YOUR THRONE 155
AUTHOR'S NOTES 157
    Mentorship of Strangers 159
    Understanding Where You Are Right Now 161
    Seeking Knowledge 164
    Knowing What to Measure 167
    Analyzing Your Business for Growth 170
    Change by Design 173
    Invisible Excellence 177
    Embracing Perspective 180
    Beyond the Breakaway 184
    Flexibility Over Fixation 188
    You Must Do or Else Nothing is Done 192
    Insights All Around Us 195
    Lead, Follow, or Get Run Over 198
    Purpose Driven Leadership 202
    A Step Toward the Throne 204
EPILOGUE 207
THANK YOU AND GODSPEED 211
ABOUT THE AUTHOR 213

THE JOURNEY

STRANDED AT THE AIRPORT

The biggest battle fought on the road to success is the one that takes place in our own minds.

In the airport lounge, sitting on a barstool, I lamented my career, my lack of direction, and my general work frustration. *Beware the High Level Dumb* continually came to mind as I pondered the wisdom of visionaries studied in business school. I don't believe that was part of the school curriculum. Sun Tzu may have imparted that sage piece of wisdom. Oh well, it doesn't matter. I have bigger problems.

Another Friday night, stranded in the Charlotte Airport! Regular work travel through the Southeastern U.S. was already wearing me down, and it was early in the year. With a heavy mental sigh, I admitted to myself it could be worse; my three-hour delayed flight to Houston could have been canceled. Maintain a positive outlook. A bright side always exists. On a whim, to get out of the noisy, rushing crowds of people and find a quiet spot in the airport, I decided to splurge on a day-pass to visit the airline lounge. So far, the lounge's peaceful atmosphere had justified its cost.

There were drinks and snacks in abundance; if I wanted something more substantial to eat, a short walk to the middle of the airport could yield decent sushi. Either way, snacks or sushi would hold me over while I wait for the flight to board in a couple of hours. Model planes circling above the sushi bar always lighten my mood. The Wright Brothers' model, in particular, is always inspiring. Focus Sam! Sun Tzu, sushi, and the Wright Brothers; pull it together and focus. I am not particularly hungry. My mind is drifting to escape the pressure of my actual problems.

I couldn't help myself. During stressful times in my life, my mind races through a myriad of random thoughts, searching for solutions that make sense of the chaos surrounding my situation at that moment. Now was one of those times; if anything, the stress was exceptionally high, and the thoughts were as fast and fleeting as trying to hold on to water racing down a mountain stream.

I should consider quitting my partnership; the thought was very appealing. Wait! What about my mortgage payment, kids' college tuition, car payments… the list is endless. Quitting is undoubtedly not a great option. I'm already making about the same amount of money I made when I worked for someone else. Moving forward towards a better life for my family and a more secure retirement was a powerful incentive for making a professional change; however, I'm not making the progress I had hoped for. I wish I had been a more attentive student in my professors' classes about compound interest and retirement planning. Ah, the mindset of the young; retirement is for old people. More than planning for retirement, few people ever mention having enough financial security in their forties to unshackle the golden handcuffs and retool into something that fulfills one's passion.

It's pointless to worry. I'm stuck and I'm going to stay stuck. Why did I ever leave my job to take over Dad's share of the company? My partnership is horrible; I'm doing all the work, getting very little credit, all the while fighting to keep Mr. Stuart's poor decisions from becoming the proverbial last nail in the coffin of my expansion dreams. How can I get out of this mess?"

My frustration and consternation did not go unnoticed by the only other person sitting in the bar area. The stranger sitting across the corner and a few stools away gently cleared his throat and smiled. "Hi, I'm Paul. You seem troubled. Are you ok?" I glanced up from my Coke-Zero to focus on Paul; he was unmistakably speaking to me, as we were the only two people in the lounge. First impression: this guy was successful in his work. Well-dressed in a blue pin-striped tailored suit, white French-cuffed shirt, silk purple tie, and light brown wingtip shoes, with that sort of style, coupled with the warm smile and kind tone of voice, Paul was most likely in sales. I wasn't interested in buying anything. Besides, we couldn't afford anything, even if we wanted what he was selling. Tapped would be the understatement of the century.

Normally, I refrain from sharing details about my life with strangers. Instead, I felt compelled by Paul's warm smile to give an honest answer. "Hi, I'm Sam. I'm a little out of sorts. Family, work, career… all of it seems to be progressing or not progressing in ways I never expected. I have degrees from top institutions, and I'm well read in virtually every area of my life; by the standards of many people, I'm what might be called… well, successful. That being said, I feel exactly the opposite."

That should make the guy run for the hills and give his co-workers a good laugh. Yes, Paul just gained a story about a crazy guy at the airport lounge. Now, my secret would be exposed; I am not a regular visitor to executive lounges. During all business trips, I fly coach to my meetings and spend extraordinarily little money on airport niceties; I only came into the lounge on a whim to escape the masses experiencing flight delays.

With a mental sigh, the pathetic nature of my words occurred to me. The average person doesn't care how you're doing, at least not in great detail; when people ask how someone is doing, it's just a way of greeting, not an invitation to data dump your life status. Even though his inquiry was uncommonly kind, Paul likely wanted to steer clear of a stranger's emotional baggage at the airport. Ironically, I undermined my own pursuit of peace and quiet.

I attempted to salvage my pride with a weak smile, hoping to lighten the atmosphere. "Excuse me, Paul, I apologize. That was too unfiltered for casual talk with a stranger. Could I revise my answer to, I'm good. My flight is delayed. Are you delayed as well?"

Then, something unexpected occurred. Paul responded with equally unfiltered honesty, "First, don't worry; your initial response likely expressed your true feelings, and I prefer being real with people. It is part of my job to keep discussions grounded in reality, regardless of the conversation topic. Second, and in the spirit of being direct and perhaps slightly comforting, it's ok; I've been where you are until discovering a better path in life. As we both have some extra time on our hands, would you like to hear about changing the rules?"

Now: Get ready, here's the sales pitch. Or was there a sales pitch? There was just something about this guy that put me at ease. So, what if there is a sales pitch in the conversation? I have at least two hours to kill, and who knows, maybe I'll learn something. With a cautiously optimistic disposition, I offered a slight shoulder shrug and replied, "Sure, tell me about changing the rules."

Paul then walked over from his seat and extended his hand. "It is nice to meet you, Sam. Mind if I sit with you?" As we shook hands, I noted his handshake was firm, but not too firm, and definitely professional. One's handshake speaks volumes regarding character. Paul's initial impression registered as engaging in every way. I gestured toward the seat in front of me. "Sure, be my guest."

Paul began by saying, "My journey through life has not been extraordinary by the standards of many people. There are no Wall Street Journal articles about me or my company; business school professors do not quote me in classes; Fortune has yet to email or call for an interview; I do not have a podcast with a million listeners; I am not rich in the conventional sense of the word; my golf score is best left unmentioned; my health is average for my age. While it's true that everything I've said is accurate, it's equally true that I offer something extraordinary to the right person. I provide a method of reimagining situations and developing more effective problem-solving strategies.

Paul stared intently into my eyes. "The perfect candidate is someone unhappy with their current life, yearning for more fulfillment. That hunger for something more could be business, family, or personal. In my humble opinion, it does not matter in the least what the area of focus might be; it matters more that there is a desire to improve one's circumstances beyond the current status. Before you run for the exit, thinking I'm a snake oil salesman, please know that what I will share is not the proverbial magical silver bullet. I do not possess all the answers for every situation or pretend to possess all the answers."

Paul continued, "My intention in sharing the information about my rather ordinary life, at least by my standards, was not to sound self-deprecating, but to convey that I am an ordinary person. Ordinary people, at least those continuing to progress through life, have made many mistakes; I have made my fair share. Those mistakes, combined with a powerful desire to learn from past errors, helped me become the person I am today. That experience shaped my self-perception, which I now summarize as a guide."

Paul seemed so comfortable sharing details about his life; it was clearly not the first time he told the story. Open discussion seems rare these days. It captured my attention and curiosity; what was it about this guy that compelled me to listen so intently?

Paul articulated, "My life path has been frustrating, depressing, joyful, and enlightening; the peaks and valleys of life are highs and lows that I experienced in the extreme. Every lesson I learned before turning forty years of age was a lesson learned the hard way. At the time each lesson was being learned, it did not feel as though the upside would be good. Mostly when experiencing a low valley, I could not envision how the upside would be an equally tall peak. One of my greatest faults is also one of my greatest assets; I am extremely stubborn. My unwillingness to surrender in the face of great adversity allowed me to conquer limitations imposed upon me by both society and myself. With the utmost conviction, I can say that at this stage in life, the latter was a more challenging peak to climb versus anything society offered as an impediment. Though not the first I learned, it has been more beneficial than most life lessons. The biggest battle fought on the road to success is the one that takes place in our own minds. It isn't until we win that battle that we can dare to hope to reach full potential in every aspect of our lives. Could I ask you a few questions so we might get to know each other a little better? Might I suggest you share some details about your career, and could you tell me where you are right now in your chosen field of work?"

Paul had already shared details about himself, so I felt obligated to share some information to fill in the blanks from my earlier comments. "I'm in Insurance. I own part of a company that was acquired from my father to facilitate his retirement and boost my career path. The latter part of that statement is the part that has troubled me. I have a background in selling manufacturing equipment. I assumed the transition would be simple, so I jumped at the chance to leave my position with a large company and be my own boss. The idea of working with Dad for a while sweetened the deal. Couple that together with the fact that my father has always earned at least twice as much as me, and you can figure out the rest. The short of it is, I am eighteen months into my partnership, and business has been stagnant. The harder we work at securing new business, the less progress it seems we make in moving the company into a more profitable position. The money I'm making is on par with what I used to make at my job; the only difference is that the stress level is now triple what it was when I was not in charge of the company. I must admit, it was a lot easier just to be responsible for selling. This management stuff is slightly more challenging than it seems when one is not managing."

"It's a frequent discovery for people moving into management," Paul confirmed with a nod. "Tell me about your education. You mentioned a couple of degrees. What was your area of study?"

He seemed to have a knack for zeroing in on frustrations sensed from my earlier comments. "I have two degrees, one in engineering and another in business. I earned my Master of Business Administration degree immediately after completing my undergraduate work. It seemed easier to keep going, and I figured the business coursework would give me an edge. That is partly why I am so frustrated about work; I should be able to solve the problems of a small business."

Paul responded, "Experiencing frustration is common. Your position is to be expected. In my opinion, after conducting research and reflecting on the topic, I believe that the average advanced degree programs in business schools effectively prepare students for prosperous careers with Fortune 500 companies, banks, and investment firms. Wall Street-guided companies hire the best students from each graduating class; some continue long-term to work for the companies, while others return to school for Master's or PhD degrees. Many fresh graduates then rejoin Wall Street-controlled companies to embark on an accelerated path to the upper echelons of leadership. National publications, newscasts, and marketing pieces showcase the leaders of companies; the program from which he or she graduated is often referenced in introductions or cited in publications and in turn fuels more applicants."

Paul continued, "If you are a little skeptical of my claim that the best and brightest are being recruited, I will concede and admit I am not referencing all the best and brightest. Many choose an alternative route, and more progressive business schools are cultivating several of those alternative routes. Some schools even offer philosophy class requirements to encourage graduates to think critically and creatively. Many programs are trying to cultivate a new generation of problem-solving graduates, rather than by-the-book, number-crunching, serve-the-shareholder-at-all-costs degree recipients. Progress is slow, and the old guard continues to grind forward."

Paul appeared to be quite sure of his opinion, and I noticed him lean forward as he explained his position on the topic: "Let us take a closer look at business education."

PROFIT BY DESIGN NOT BY DEGREE

The true measure of business education isn't your starting salary, it's your ability to solve real problems.

With a matter-of-fact note in his voice, Paul said, "If one reads job posting boards or scans Human Resources sections of most company websites, it is easy to find verbiage referencing best, top-notch, high performers, high-class rank, and top-scoring applicants should apply. I've seen no Fortune 500 job postings seeking merely adequate candidates. The top business schools understand this process and play the game of recruiting students and placing workers quite well. They market this as Return on Investment or ROI."

Paul continued, "Each year, many national publications and universities publish data on the average salary of MBA or other advanced degree graduates. It is a powerful recruiting tool. Not sure? I would challenge you to ask the average MBA student from any top 100 program in the United States what percentage of graduates from their program are hired within one year of graduation and the average starting salary before bonuses; the average student will most assuredly offer an answer very close to the figures published by their respective school. Many will offer statistics related to competing programs. One thing you will rarely hear about is the number of graduates who become the President or CEO of a new or acquired company. Those statistics are less prominently displayed, if displayed at all, because they lower the average stated salary; this would emphasize a lower return on investment (ROI) of tuition. When you consider that the average tuition for a top-tier MBA program exceeds $100,000, it is easy to understand why universities might be hesitant to promote or share negative information. This is flawed thinking by those, shall we say, less than progressive programs."

I chimed in, "Yes, I think you are right. Students in my MBA program were excited about recruiting days. The school facilitated company visits, job fairs, and mixers. I do not recall a single event dedicated to students launching businesses or securing funding for a new venture. While I often read about entrepreneur-related events or services happening in schools today, it was not part of the curriculum when I attended my program. I was always worried about getting a decent job. I never envisioned leading a small firm. My dream was to be CEO of a big company."

With a sagely nod, Paul showed his understanding. "That was, and sadly remains, the core challenge of many programs. This is unfortunate because many large organizations have been downsizing in recent years; as a result, many employees have chosen to leave the corporate world and start small businesses. Many are not prepared for the challenges of ownership. The Small Business Administration reports that small businesses account for approximately 55% of all U.S. sales. Even with these impressive numbers, large businesses still control the headlines of nightly news and most financial publications."

My corporate pride kicked in for a moment, and I interjected, "It sounds like you're jaded toward big business and higher education in America. After all, big businesses did not start as big businesses. Unless I am mistaken, most started as small businesses with the dream and willpower of an owner or group of owners propelling the company to the heights of big business."

Paul's reply, delivered with a smile, was: "Actually, the opposite is true of my feelings toward big business, and especially universities. I am definitely not jaded; I am not against big business, so much as I am a huge proponent of small business. In recent years, universities' creation of entrepreneurship concentrations in their business schools has been a very encouraging development in the higher education industry."

Paul added, "Such programs, especially their leadership training, best serve my small business clients. The stories of small business owners who became big business owners offer precisely the fascinating case studies that motivate people studying business. It makes for great classroom discussion and excellent television fodder. Unmentioned and often overlooked is the significant number of startups in business sectors that either fail or underperform. Alas, the bootstrap startup growing into a behemoth company is the type of case study not of great interest to me, as they neither encourage nor motivate me, nor many of those I serve."

I had often thought along that same line of reasoning; it is excellent for them, but what does that have to do with me? I nodded. "I agree, Paul. While that sort of story makes for interesting reading, my business is unlikely to grow into a billion-dollar company. I am more interested in not failing and making a profit than becoming the dominant story on social media. What interests you if those kinds of case studies don't appeal to you? Perhaps my situation may benefit from considering alternative information."

Paul leaned in a little and declared, "Exactly. You are now thinking along the right lines. I had the same thought and started looking for inspiration within the different scenarios; the story behind or within the story became the objective of my research. The change in how some companies manage their internal divisions has caught my interest. In particular, how some large businesses assign profit-and-loss responsibility to division or department managers is beneficial in virtually every way. In this kind of setting, a person needs to regard their part of the business as a company. In this pseudo company, the firm has clients, the cost of goods or services required to produce their products or services, and expenses related to labor, communications, supplies, and other line items typical of a company. This autonomy and responsibility might make managers rethink efficient work practices and improved client service."

Paul continued to share his opinion, "I believe, in most cases, the clients are internal to the organization. By considering other company divisions as vendors or customers, and focusing on the importance of relationships, the organization benefits from improved retention, stronger relationships, and increased revenue. This method is not without problems. Managers may utilize internal suppliers, although better outside choices exist. Or superior strategies for growth or efficiency might be shelved because they do not align with the overarching company's business plan. Does this line of reasoning seem to gel with your experience in either a larger company or in your own small business?"

Paul's insightful take on higher education and big business presented an interesting argument for how the business world honestly operates. My own experiences supported his arguments.

"You argue some interesting points. Your business school analysis is difficult to dispute, especially considering past practices. It seems that my situation, in particular, serves as evidence that the traditional programs of the past were indeed somewhat lacking in creating small business problem solvers. The sad part of this conversation for me is that while we agree that modern-day business programs, or at least the better programs, are offering training in precisely my area of greatest challenge, I am a bit too old to return to school. Even if it would greatly benefit me, I lack the time and desire to enroll in a program. What's the solution for someone in my position? Are you suggesting I abandon my work and pursue another business degree?"

Paul seemed to sense my trepidation regarding such a drastic life change and offered, "No, I am not suggesting you quit your job to return to school. While I am a fan of higher education and believe you could benefit from more education, you already possess the foundational level of business acumen needed to succeed. In short, more formal education is not what you need. A guiding strategy for you and your company's progress seems to be missing. And now we have reached the crux of what services I provide; I specialize in helping people, specifically people working in small businesses, develop a workable, ever-evolving strategy that allows them to fulfill their dreams."

CHANGING THE LENS

*A strategy model should
always be working.*

    I thought about what Paul had just said, ultimately concluding that the guy was not suggesting something outlandish. There is no way for me to quit what I am doing right now to attend school. I value lifelong learning, but I prefer to learn independently at my own pace. Another degree is probably not in my future.

    I felt a little more comfortable continuing the conversation. "What do you mean by ever-evolving? Is that some new age type of thing I missed in school?"

    Paul responded, "No. You did not miss that strategy class in school. Allow me to explain. What I mean is that strategy models should always be working. Envision a strategy model as a document or idea that directs everyday choices to meet customer and business requirements best, concurrently maximizing customer satisfaction and company earnings. If that sounds too good to be true, perhaps it is time for you and your company to follow a different model."

Paul seemed to sense my interest. "Before you reply, consider how many hard-working people you know or have heard of who invested their life savings and many hours per week for multiple decades only to close when a big superstore-type retailer physically or virtually moved to town?"

I replied, "I know many company owners who closed in recent years when big competition moved to town or people started buying more products online to be shipped to their homes. I also know that is part of my struggle. My father was able to compete and steadily grow the company during his years of ownership; no matter how hard or smart I try to work, duplicating his results has proved challenging."

"Did those owners you know retire comfortably, or did they go back to work?" Paul wondered. "What I mean is, were they essentially forced out of business? Further to my point, and I believe we both know the answer to the question: was the small business closing the fault of the competing big box superstores, or should it rest more rightly with the small business owner? Indeed, in the scenario I mentioned, the small business owner might have had a thirty-year advantage in that market."

I let his words sink in for a moment. I have always felt that many people prefer to blame others instead of taking responsibility for their own actions; people often blame Wall Street, the government, competitors, foreign businesses, labor laws, or any other scapegoat that is currently in the spotlight. That way of thinking never appealed to me. I believe people are worth what they are worth in virtually every situation. If you want to be worth more to your family, invest time with your spouse and kids. Taking them for granted never works. Add value if you want to be worth more to your company or customers. Whatever the area of life, the solution seemed simple: add value. Those who add value through revenue, efficiency, relationships, or whatever seem to enjoy greater success.

In my previous job, my salary provided a steady stream of income. Still, it was the commissions that enabled me to contribute financially enough to buy a house and support my family. I added value by selling more than most of my teammates through the long-lasting relationships that resulted in repeat orders year after year. Rather than always thinking of getting the next deal, I focused on taking care of those investing time and money in the current deal. The next deal was always there, usually with the same customer.

It seemed difficult to find any fault in Paul's argument. "I get what you are saying. My guiding principle: add value, then let things unfold. This has worked great for many years of my life. The challenge is that while I have enjoyed business success in the past and expect continued success in my personal relationships, I am struggling to add value for my customers. Maybe this is the core reason our business isn't growing."

Paul nodded and said, "Adding value is important in every business I have examined. Businesses often add value by providing a product or service that is faster, cheaper, better, or more efficient from the customer's perspective. Note the operative words from the customer's perspective. The customer's experience and opinion of value are what matter. A guiding rule shared with me long ago is that reputation perceived is thusly achieved, good or bad, as the case may be."

Maybe adding value is something I no longer understand. Is it just a price game now? Is my current industry just a commodity to be shopped online, or is there some hope? With a hushed sigh and a weak voice, I confessed, "I am so very frustrated."

Paul smiled warmly as he glanced toward the hallway. "Hey, I have been where you are until I changed my position of perception. I had a little help in that area. Now, speaking of that help, here she comes."

I looked up to see a smartly dressed woman walking towards us. Light gray suit, professionally accented jewelry, and shoes my wife would love. She moved with the calm confidence of someone who didn't need to prove anything. Her presence felt intentional, like someone who had found what I was still looking for. She smiled and offered a wave as she approached Paul. She leaned towards him, kissing his cheek and briefly hugging him. He responded in kind, and she then turned towards me with a smile and said, "Hi, my name is Gennie, Paul's wife. Is he intruding upon your quiet time in the lounge? I can reign him in if you like." She said that with a little upturned corner of her mouth, which let me know she teased him for our mutual benefit.

"Hi, I'm Sam," I said while extending my hand in greeting. She offered her hand, and as we shook hands, I noticed that her handshake was firm but not too firm and definitely professional. My first impression of Gennie was that she was as sharp as her style of dress and every bit as confident as Paul appeared; they seemed like a splendid match.

Resuming our seats, I clarified, "Paul was sharing insightful viewpoints on small businesses. He was the uplifting part of the conversation and, if anything, I took up his time by sharing some of my burdensome thoughts concerning business frustrations." I offered a weak smile and continued, "Paul was just saying he experienced many of the same business frustrations I am dealing with in my insurance business until his outlook changed. He also said you were responsible for changing his perspective."

Gennie looked directly into my eyes, spoke confidently, and said, "Yes, it is absolutely true; Paul was as lost as a ball in high weeds when we met." She laughed a warm laugh and smiled, which let me know this must be some long-standing joke between them. She said, "I'm allowed to use cute little sayings, as I was born and raised in West Texas. It seems to translate wherever we travel in the U.S., so I hang onto little things like colloquialisms from my childhood that are applicable to life today. How about you, where are you from?"

I replied, "I spent most of my childhood in Southern Virginia. My family moved to Houston when I was in college, so Texas became home. After school, I got a job and stayed. As many people say, and I am sure you will appreciate, I wasn't born in Texas, but got there as fast as I could!"

Gennie laughed softly and with a mirthful smile said, "I do indeed appreciate that comment. Paul is a transplant too, and I refuse to hold it against him. It is nice to know a few details about people. So often people hurry to and fro, never making eye contact while passing, and live their lives day after day with little interaction. The pleasantries take such a small amount of time, but add in ways we may or may not see in the moment. My inclination is to view them as ripples in a pond, traveling ever outward, transmitting cheer. We could discuss that later; you were about to talk about perspective. Should we continue? Catch me up in the conversation, please."

I smiled and began summarizing my story. "I'm happy to do so, although happy is not a word I will use to describe my situation. Sadly, I feel depressed and frustrated. The condensed version is that I used to sell manufacturing equipment. My father retired, and I took over his portion of the insurance business. I have a loving and very patient wife, two kids, and a dog. Formal education includes two degrees, one of which is in business. We are ok financially; many would say I'm living the American dream. My frustration mostly stems from a stable business and my ineffective approach to addressing challenges that would enable real growth and progress. Despite success in sales and basic business knowledge, I am at a loss on how to proceed."

Gennie absorbed that momentarily and said, "First, let me congratulate you on admitting your challenges. It is hard for many people to admit they need help. It sounds as though you understand that needing a little help is ok. Collaboration can be powerful. That is a great initial step. Second, I agree with the direction of conversation with Paul regarding perspective. Point of view counts for a lot in business, more than most people seem to realize."

Gennie then said, "Paul and I have different business backgrounds. Our story began when we met at a business conference. I was in real estate sales and interested in other opportunities. Paul was already in consulting, focusing on big companies and placing five- to ten-person teams on consulting assignments for extended periods. We began a conversation at a morning coffee chat session that continued into the afternoon. The abbreviated version is that our frustration with current positions in the workforce, coupled with a belief that we could help people solve problems, led to further discussions. Those additional conversations sparked a personal and professional interest, ultimately leading to our marriage and the creation of our consulting company. We specialize in coaching small business leaders to develop and execute successful company strategies, thereby helping them achieve their goals. When I say business, I mean it in an all-inclusive way. Perspective applies to all aspects of the respective companies, including, but not limited to, customers, clients, sustainability, technology, goals, and evaluation."

Gennie continued, "Step one, when we formed the company, was to decide on a model we would use to help people. Despite our collective experience and education, we were unaware of, or could not find, a solid business strategy model for small businesses. We searched for basic business plans and found many layouts and examples, none of which seemed to include all the areas we knew to be necessary to manage a company; searches for strategy models yielded results that seemed more applicable to large companies. Ultimately, there was always something missing. Sometimes, business plans do not include a competitive analysis; in other instances, there is no indication of what initial steps a leader might take to implement the strategy. As I said, there just always seemed to be something missing. Our research surprised us. In short, we'd written business plans, developed strategies for our own and other businesses, and even mentored others in strategic planning and business development. How had we missed it? Our surprise and disbelief fueled our drive to create a model that makes sense for small business owners."

With my obvious interest showing, I said, "Ok, I admit I am intrigued. Perhaps there is a better way to manage my company. If you wouldn't mind, I'd like to hear more about this strategy model." As they began to explain what they had created, I felt something shift. Maybe there was a different way to think about business. Perhaps the way forward wasn't about working harder, but working smarter, with a strategy that worked.

THE THRONE OF PROFIT

A company exists in perpetual limbo, resting somewhere between success and failure, without a properly developed strategic plan.

Gennie gestured towards the bar area. "What do you see when you look at those barstools?"

"When I look at the barstools, I believe it may be a nice place to sit while idling a few minutes away before boarding my next flight."

She then nodded towards the bar area again. "Look closer. Each barstool has three legs. The importance of the three legs is pretty clear; if one leg is missing or shorter than the others, the stool wobbles or falls.

Visualize the barstool as your business throne of profit. Strategy, Action, and Measurement are the labels for the three legs. If you want to sit on a throne of profit, meaning you want a company to produce stable or growing profit, all three legs must be high-functioning. Each of the three is a model; those three models combined are what we call the **Throne of Profit System**™."

I let my mind process that for a minute and then said, "I believe I understand. One without the other two doesn't work. Or does it? I know many companies, including mine, that are open and generating a profit; perhaps not as much as I would like, but still profitable. I am fairly certain my company could exist like this for many years; always generating as much income as I had in my job, but maybe never performing as well as I would like."

Paul chimed in, "And that is the point. Companies can exist for many years, perhaps generations, without closing. A company that exists without closing, while not generating profit, is not much of a company. Simply stated, companies like that sound more like a hobby than a business. If that sounds a little harsh, we could phrase it differently; the best explanation that can be offered is that the owner created a job. Just because a business has been, or is, functioning that way, does not mean it has to function that way forever."

There was truth in those words; I needed that sort of truth in my thought process if I planned to move my current business situation into the profitable column. Languishing in our current state would only end in failure; perhaps not the failure of the business, but the failure of me achieving my dreams for what the company could be and the life it could create for my family. Wasting time and energy to be average, or just creating a job for myself, was unappealing.

Gennie laughed, winked, and said, "That is true. If it weren't true, we would be out of work. And that would be unfortunate. Let's take a closer look at what we mean by strategy."

ToP Strategy Model™:

Gennie continued, "Much like the **Throne of Profit System™** I described using the barstool, three legs make up a good strategy model: Analysis, Vision, and Goals. Analysis without vision or goals is more akin to an academic exercise than good planning. If a vision lacks thorough planning or skips intermediate steps, it's unlikely to succeed. It's pointless to set a goal without considering how to achieve it. As we understand it, strategy serves three specific purposes for small businesses. First, management must have a holistic understanding of the company's current position. Second, and building upon the first purpose, leadership can purposefully envision the company's future position. Ultimately, the culmination of the aforementioned steps should result in the translation of the vision into focused goals that bridge the gap between today and tomorrow. Make sense?"

It seemed to make sense to me. I replied, "It makes sense. I feel rather compelled to say it also sounds pretty simple. I do not mean simple in a derogatory way; it is more that I understand what you mean, and it resonates with my beliefs about achieving things in life or business. Please tell me briefly what you mean by Analysis, Vision, and Goals. I want to be sure I'm clear in my understanding."

Gennie then shared her perspective on what makes up business analysis. It was over my head, or at least in the moment, it was too much to take in. The overall concept was clear to me; however, the details presented posed a greater challenge.

"That is a lot to take in," I softly said, exhaling a long, slow breath. Gennie smiled and said, "Yes. Yes, it is. That is why it is so important to develop a strategy properly."

Paul chimed in and said, "Without working through the development of a plan in a way that results in setting a series of goals, a company exists in perpetual limbo, resting somewhere between success and failure. More often than is necessary, companies will then gravitate towards the latter. Not planning properly begets failure."

"That makes sense. I never thought of planning as something that resulted in a defined goal or series of goals, yet I can see the logic in thinking of strategy as planning or a goal creation exercise." Paul and Gennie both nodded, and I continued, "Assuming I go through the process of creating a plan that results in goals, what then?"

Paul leaned back in the chair, looked at me piercingly, and said, "You act."

Gennie then rejoined and added, "That means more than most people think it does when contemplating business decisions. Acting on goals can be challenging, so much so that action never happens as it relates to particular goals or initiatives. Remember, the concept of strategy creation involves holistically considering the company's current position, enabling leadership to envision its future position and create goals that bridge the current and future states. The next part of a strategic business model is indeed acting. Remember what we discussed earlier: there are three key components to a successful strategic business plan. The creation of the strategy is one of the three legs of the barstool. We label the second part "action." I'll let Paul explain."

ToP Action Model™:

Paul leaned in; his passion was evident: "People often form splendid plans, yet stop the process at the point of plan creation. Why not act? Is it the fear of failure or success? Is the collective knowledge not sufficient to enable enough understanding to act? Is there a shortage of money or other available resources? Is the risk viewed as too great? Is the return on investment deemed too little versus the risk? What is the real reason for not acting? Leaders must proactively address challenges and overcome obstacles hindering progress to ensure continued company growth and profitability. This is the fundamental reason for taking action."

Paul continued, "A company just sustaining operations in today's competitive environment means falling further behind competing businesses month after month, year after year. Whatever the challenge hindering the continual accomplishment of immediate, short-term, and long-term goals associated with the strategy may be, the leader or leaders of a company must endeavor to remove or limit those challenges. If the challenge for a company is a lack of knowledge, investing time, money, or both to overcome the shortage essentially means hiring, renting, or developing it. If the challenge is money, earn or borrow enough to achieve the desired result. Strategies that work in a startup's initial stages may prove ineffective once revenues reach two or three million dollars. Whatever the situation, this is a core management responsibility; ignoring this responsibility is folly."

Gennie then said, "Pay close attention, as this is vital. First, leaders of a business must act with purpose. Deciding to act upon a strategy or plan helps a business move forward efficiently and profitably. The savings of time and resources are especially crucial for small businesses; making a hundred-thousand-dollar mistake in a business generating a billion dollars annually in revenue is barely noticeable; a hundred-thousand-dollar error, even one that is annualized out over five years, could be the difference between a profitable small business and one forced to close. Second, being purposeful leads to actions that capitalize on one's strengths. Taking advantage of strengths, or what business schools refer to as core competencies, creates a natural competitive edge. Finally, the result of being purposeful in your choices and working primarily in areas of competitive strength is getting it right. Mistakes in small businesses are especially costly. It is much more cost-effective, meaning saving time and money, to take sound action once than to haphazardly act, create a problem, and invest resources to fix the challenge created by poor choices. Act with purpose, play to strengths, and get it right the first time."

ToP Measurement Model™:

Paul then spoke, "Let's talk a little about measurement and what that means. Mastering your financials is vital to success. Don't be intimidated! If this is not an area with which you have a lot of confidence or understanding, take a class on QuickBooks, either online or using local educational resources. If that idea is unappealing, consider hiring a bookkeeper or an accounting service that will meet your needs for monthly reporting in a way that allows you to track your company's progress. Mastering the quantitative aspect of the business allows the owner to focus on mastering the qualitative portion of leading the company towards greater success."

He continued, "Segmentation of revenue, cost of goods sold, expenses, and profit is a good foundational way to look at financials. This doesn't preclude the existence of beneficial subcategories within those large areas. It means this is a sound starting point for quickly evaluating company performance. Leadership within a company should minimally know each month how the company is trending in each of those key areas. In short, is the company progressing, sustaining, or reducing in a way that is aligned with immediate, short-, or long-term goals?"

Paul then slowed the pace of his words, intimating that this point was perhaps even more vital than most others. "Trending is a new concept for most small business owners; a little more explanation is probably needed to allow an understanding of what we mean. Small business does not equal big business. Waiting for a quarterly report or, worse yet, waiting until the October following the previous year to get a copy of the tax documents filed to meet your extension deadline, before knowing if you made or lost money, is unlikely to yield favorable results. While interesting, comparing a small business owner's performance from the previous month to the same month last year does not provide a basis for making better decisions for today or tomorrow. The same applies to comparing data from one year with that of the previous year. It is too slow and does not effectively reinforce good decisions or quickly reveal poor ones, so an owner or manager cannot course-correct the company almost immediately. A better way to judge a company's progress is to look at running twelve-month data sets.

This means taking annualized profit-and-loss statements, the most recent twelve months, and comparatively evaluating that data as it relates to at least six previous data sets."

Gennie then looked at me and said, "Does that make sense to you, Sam? Small businesses must act fast, adapt, improvise, and overcome. Waiting to evaluate wins and losses for any extended period is counterproductive. One or two months is not enough time to meet a long-term strategic goal, but within that period, we can measure incremental progress. The wins acknowledged by recognizing and celebrating minor steps on the path of progress help keep owners and stakeholders on that path. This is especially true if they implemented a new method or system. It is hard to notice revenue, cost of goods sold, expenses, or profit changing by half of a percentage point up or down because of an operational decision; if plotted or evaluated each month, slight changes are very noticeable."

Gennie continued, "The trap owners and employees alike often fall into when making a change is by failing to recognize when wins are happening. They, in turn, fail to celebrate the incremental successes, and slipping back into old habits becomes the common norm. Realizing trends motivates the continuous evaluation of good and bad decisions, leading to actions that can positively affect the company."

I sat for a minute, trying to absorb everything they were discussing, pondering the meaning of many words and how all the concepts worked together. I was sure I had learned a lot about thinking differently about my business and business in general, but I was unsure of the depth or extent of those thoughts. Paul and Gennie were looking at me, waiting for the look of acknowledgement, understanding, hope, fear, I am not sure what exactly. "Gennie, Paul, that was beyond enlightening, perhaps even a little perplexing, but a lot to consider. I am unsure what to say except thank you for sharing your thoughts. My thoughts are swirling, and I feel you gifted me with a lot of knowledge, and I need some time to think about all you said." As my phone buzzed with the flight notification, I realized it was time to board the flight.

Our time in the lounge was over. After thanking them for sharing some time and exchanging contact information, we parted ways. So much had been said during our conversation that it was almost too much to absorb in a single interaction. One thought dominated: perspective is essential. I needed to adapt.

WHEN EFFORT ISN'T ENOUGH

There is a better way to work than just logging more hours at the office.

A few weeks had passed since I met Paul and Gennie at the airport. Almost every encounter with a business associate since then brought parts of that conversation to mind; real-life case studies, if you will, for examining my new perspective. I'll never forget that night. As soon as I boarded the plane and found my seat, I pulled out my notebook and began taking notes. I spent the entire flight from Charlotte to Houston writing down every detail I could remember from our exchange. I'm sure I missed a few things or jumbled others, but I captured what I could. I couldn't stop thinking about business in a new way.

That was when I decided to become more intentional in my meetings. I made it a goal to see longtime clients and business contacts with fresh eyes. I reached out to Jimmy, a lifelong friend and real estate agent who owned his firm, and invited him to join me for a round of golf. He gladly accepted.

Jimmy and I finished our round of golf and decided to soften the blow of our poor scores with a drink at the clubhouse. It was the perfect early afternoon; the wind offered a slight breeze to make the lower eighties temperature feel perfect; the sun was getting a little lower in the sky, and the putting green was empty except for a few remaining practice balls left for the course staff to retrieve as the day ended. Jimmy suggested we enjoy our beverages on the patio overlooking the putting green; I heartily agreed, and we made our way towards the seats near the corner so as not to be disturbed during our conversation.

Settling into our seats, we clinked glasses, a familiar ritual, before I asked, "How's the office treating you?"

Jimmy answered, "Things are fairly good considering the market. Nationally, the housing market shows improvement in new home sales and stability in existing ones. Locally, we hold our own against other large to mid-sized firms. That is a bit concerning as I do not think I could work more hours in a week. This is my first time taking time for myself in two months. Because I want to be transparent with an old friend, I admit I feel a little guilty for playing golf for a few hours on Saturday. I only decided to play, and not cancel, because I knew we'd be discussing business during the afternoon. Furthermore, I hoped, and continue to hope, to gain something from the exchange. I typically leave our meetings feeling encouraged, enlightened, or both."

I replied, "I understand what you mean, Jimmy. I work a lot of hours myself, and taking time to golf and share an afternoon with a friend carries an equal mixture of guilt and relief. Perhaps we can help each other a little to improve our respective businesses; sharing ideas on how to make things better might be beneficial for both of us. I trust you to keep our conversation confidential, and I hope you feel the same trust and believe I will keep our discussion confidential."

He affirmed, "Of course."

I continued, "Golf is a fun distraction and seems to take my mind off the myriad of challenges each day offers, but those same challenges are always there the next day. I believe there is a better way to work than just logging more hours at the office."

Jimmy nodded while sipping a little of his drink, then said, "I couldn't agree more. Despite my agreement, I'm short on solutions. The harder I work, the harder my competition works. If it is slow for me, it is slow for them too; feast or famine is the little saying we use in the real estate business to describe the ups and downs of the market. I have yet to learn how to smooth out the lows and take advantage of the highs."

Feeling a little like Jimmy's situation might be like mine, and helping him find a solution might help illuminate my thinking, I asked, "What do you use for information to examine the market? Earlier, you said that new home sales were improving, while existing home sales remained stable. Where did you get that information?"

Jimmy sat still for a moment and considered the question, then said, "Well, Sam, I have to admit my response consisted mostly of the typical rhetoric gleaned from exchanges at local real estate agent gatherings, conversations with customers, and listening to the nightly news. That information generally correlates with my sales, and whenever someone asks how things are going with the market, I parrot back whatever I have heard recently."

His reply, formulated from unsound data, or a dearth of it, seemed to disappoint him a little. Recognizing this seemed genuine, I used the pause and continued, "Your reaction suggests you might be ignoring real market data for rumors. Don't feel bad. Hearing you offer your answer and pushing a little to where we are now in the conversation, it has become evident that I do the same thing."

"What is the solution? What can help us?" Jimmy asked with a small sigh. "It sounds like we could both use a better understanding of our markets."

Nodding in agreement, I offered, "I agree. While on a trip a while back, I met some interesting people who suggested it was essential to analyze your business to improve planning. They explained that analysis means understanding all your available resources. You can accomplish this by assessing your Resources, Market, and Delivery of goods or services. Resources are best thought of as having three focus areas: Financial, Operational, and People-oriented. Examining your market involves assessing your Company and the Micro and Macro factors that drive business. They also discussed examining Delivery by examining your Marketing, Logistics, and Service. If that seems like a lot to absorb, trust me when I tell you it was too much for me to understand when I first heard it. I've pondered that part of our conversation, and I'm still unsure I fully comprehend what they meant. Still, it gave me a framework to consider where my company stands versus other firms and the market."

After pausing to let the wealth of information sink in, Jimmy smiled faintly and remarked, "That's quite a lot to process. Admittedly, I commonly examine two financial areas to understand my status when considering my current situation. I examine my checking account balance and the number of pending deals in the office to predict my income for the next couple of months. Things are either going okay with the office and staff, or I make changes. Anything more complex or analytical, as a thought about how things are with the company, is not part of what I would consider my normal course of business. That's not to say what you're sharing is invalid; it's more a concession on my part of what I now believe is a shortcoming in my management style. I own a company, yet I live paycheck to paycheck; if I stopped working for two months, my business would start to need savings or a small loan to keep it afloat. That wasn't my intention when I started this company."

I thought for a second about how similar our situations were and said, "Tell me about when you started. I know the story, but I want to hear it again.

After all these years, my perspective might be slightly different, and sharing some details of the early years could help me better understand my situation."

With a straighter posture and a transformed expression, Jimmy happily began narrating his company's history. "The best point to start is at the beginning because it tells so much about where my mind was during that time in my life. I was young and fearless; ah, the glory of youth is fleeting. The day I opened my company is as clear to me 20 years later as it was the day I decided to forge a different path in my life. I was on the front walkway of a competing brokerage, discussing a transaction with another real estate agent. It was a sweltering day in the middle of July, and temperatures were soaring, literally and figuratively, as we debated the finer points of a contract."

He continued, "I represented the buyer, and the other agent represented the seller. The other agent's name was Joan. After a little back and forth, Joan moved to end the debate by stating, I have twenty years of experience, and you need to understand how business works. If the seller agrees to do the repairs, the buyer should proceed with the purchase. Your people are not doing things as they should be, and you should guide them better. It is in the seller's best interest to close this deal; after all, the seller is paying the commission. You and I should work together to ensure the deal gets done and we get to the closing table. That is how we earn a commission from the people paying us in this deal."

Jimmy, now on a roll and telling the story with vigor. "I was fuming and informed her that the transaction creates the deal, and in our state, Buyer Agency was now a matter of law. Furthermore, and to that very point, my actions were in the buyer's best interest. The laws regarding representation have recently changed. Although that wasn't how business had been transacted for the last twenty years while she was getting her experience, this was indeed how real estate was practiced today. Perhaps a few continuing education classes could bring her up to speed to where I was in my understanding of how transactions work."

"In hindsight, I could have communicated that differently," Jimmy said, "but her condescending tone made me angry. Because I was feeling offended, I launched an aggressive counterattack. On a positive note, once she realized I couldn't be bullied, we gained a mutual respect and closed several deals over the years. It was an excellent lesson on how to stand my ground for a client, and I left the exchange with a newfound purpose: to open a firm where agents are trained, motivated, and supervised. I would promote doing business the right way, meaning always operating in the very best interest of the clients. My thought was, and still is, that by looking out for those we serve first, the other things will fall into place easily along the way. I still think that is the right way to do business."

Jimmy continued, "I left that meeting and opened my first office within the next ninety days. I was so motivated to launch the company that I secured licensure from the state, took possession of the new office space, and only then realized I didn't have a phone system or furniture ordered for use in the new office. Smooth business moves; yes sir. You should respect my business prowess."

Jimmy smirked. "That was how I operated in the early days; ten steps forward, nine back, start again on an alternate path. Eventually, I solved the challenges of opening a business and made it function despite my many blunders."

For a time, Jimmy shared a narrative encompassing the company's early hiring successes and failures, including the firing of employees, fluctuations in customer base, and crucial transactions that contributed to its prosperity. His pride was inspiring.

CHANGE WITH THE TIMES

Hope does not equal a business plan.

    Jimmy's account of his journey, from the walkway in front of a competitor's office to where he is today, impressed me. Although he was not number one in the market, I knew his peers respected him. I had heard as much at some of the civic group meetings I attended each month. Perhaps I was so impressed because it was only now, given my current situation, that I could relate to and appreciate the courage it takes to make those early moves. Although my father and his partner founded our company, our current position more closely resembles that of a startup than an established firm. My company's success was contingent on considerable improvements. Unsure what exactly might help me with a breakthrough, I eagerly listened.

As he continued sharing his story, I became excited by his revelation regarding the analysis of his company's current position, which seemed parallel to my own circumstances. I said, "Jimmy, my business is the same. Although I didn't start the way you did, our current situation is remarkably similar. I work hard, pay bills, and meet payroll for both myself and the staff; the company is doing okay. That does not mean I could lay aside my responsibilities for any period and expect the company to thrive without me."

I continued, "My newfound way of thinking is I have more of a job than a business. I could work my job from now until I am no longer able to work. It will provide a solid living and lots of pleasure; the challenge is that I dream of it being more. As you know, my father sold me his share of the business; I hope to one day do the same thing and sell my share of the company to a buyer. Disclosing your thoughts, successes, and struggles reinforces my opinion on how I need to operate in the future, meaning I need to do a better job of figuring out where the company stands in terms of resources, market, and delivery. My thinking is becoming more organized."

Jimmy declared, "I think we should get together for a regular game of golf. If I got nothing else from the exchange today than a sense of urgency regarding how I look at my company, I think the firm will be in a better position in the future. I have spent most of my life working hard and trying to provide better service than my competition; that was okay initially, but business is changing. There are additional needs with social media, web-based advertising, apps, AI, responding to customers, and prospecting for new sales associates; I am a sales guy, not all of the roles I just mentioned. My current staff, while good at what they currently do, are not equipped to take the company beyond our current market ranking. Now that I'm thinking about it, our customers deserve more. People count on us to help them with one of their biggest financial decisions: buying or selling a home. If I allow the company to be less than we can be, I have failed as an owner. If any of that sounds even slightly negative, I apologize; my feelings are the opposite, as I feel energized to make improvements. I really need to work on my business, instead of working in my business all of the time."

Jimmy's level of excitement was evident and caused me a bit of concern, so I offered, "What do you think you will do to make changes? Are you going to fire all of your employees and hire a bunch of kids fresh out of college?"

With a little chuckle, he said, "No. I don't think I will go into the office on Monday and fire the staff. I think there might be a better option. As I sit here, thinking about how business is ever-changing and how my company should adapt to the times, it has occurred to me that perhaps we should continually improve through training. Loyalty and experience are hard to replace in my business. Until a person has held an open house on a Sunday afternoon when the temperature was 100°F, with no air conditioning because the builder had inspection troubles during the week and could not complete the installation, it is hard to discuss frustrations agents have about holding future open houses. Although the logic of holding houses open on the weekend will make sense to an agent, the emotional side of that same person reeling from the frustration of a hot afternoon with no prospects coming to visit is hard to overcome unless you empathize.

The same goes for the staff, people who handle our marketing and take incoming calls; personality is hard to teach. Responses that are genuine and sound empathetic are hard to replicate unless they are, well, authentic. Not that young people cannot express genuine concern for another person; in fact, I believe the opposite. Still, for the average person, I think it is easier to empathize with a family struggling with a move if your own family has felt some of the same pain, inconvenience, and stress with a prior housing situation. Make sense?"

"Yes, it does," I offered with a nod of understanding. "I have interacted with people in the past who appeared clueless about challenges I was facing with the delivery of a product within the timeline I promised a customer. I can think of many instances that caused great frustration in my old role, when I promised to deliver a product by a certain deadline to a customer, only to have people within my organization threaten to extend that timeline. I felt stressed when I had to explain why that specific order required a heightened sense of urgency. The promised deadline was for a reason; the customer agreed to pay for expedited delivery for a reason. The customer and I expected the deadline to be met."

I continued, "Some people in my old organization behaved as though anything out of the normal operating procedure should be called into question and was a source of inconvenience. Frustrated, our division's vice president would often exclaim to anyone outside sales: Without customers, you don't have any paperwork! The emails they respond to, the orders they process, and the paycheck they get in the form of direct deposit every other week would not happen if sales did not happen. What about that is hard to understand? I agreed with her position, and after many years of working together and numerous conversations about the attitudes of those around us that did not align with our department's values, we developed a camaraderie related to our long-suffering positions between the customers and those with the company-only-needs-the-company mindset. Some people understand sales, while others do not."

"I agree one hundred percent," Jimmy said. "In my business, if you don't *get it* when it comes to customer wants and needs, you will forever be steps behind those in the business who can empathize and make connections on an emotional level. Sympathizing does not equal empathizing! The two are vastly different."

We touched upon several other local events before Jimmy remembered his family dinner and departed. As we parted ways, I wondered if he would use our conversation as a catalyst for gaining a new perspective about his company. I stayed a few minutes longer, enjoying the quiet solitude and pondering the company's analysis process.

Jimmy seemed no different from me in terms of the lack of a deep analysis of our respective companies;

passing thoughts on how things stand right now with the checking account, issues with current employees, or tweaking something here and there in response to a problem seemed the norm. I doubt that the way of practicing business is hugely different for many people. The grind of doing business that way felt increasingly like a job, rather than working to build something.

Where is Jimmy's company going? Where is my company going, for that matter? I'm not sure Jimmy has an answer other than he wants to be number one in the market; being number one in a market seems unlikely to happen by accident or luck. The longer I sat thinking about analyzing a company, the more convinced I became that if a company could potentially create the opportunity to be number one in any market, its leaders needed a strong understanding of the current status. The conversation with Paul and Gennie made more sense with each passing moment.

I need to break down my situation into bite-sized pieces I can digest and gain a better understanding. Competitors are strong today, and much of the playing field is leveled; it is no longer enough to work hard and hope for the best. *Hope does not equal a business plan.* I could work hard for the rest of my life, but what would it accomplish? As I pondered the plethora of potential answers, a quote from Peter Drucker came to mind. "The best way to predict the future is to create it."

That quote seemed profound many years ago when I read it in business school. Although Ducker's genius faded from the forefront of my business vocabulary over the years, his wisdom seemed incredibly apropos during my respite on the patio. I need to revisit key business works and arm myself with a fresh perspective.

With reluctance, I admitted how far off the mark from being a lifelong learner I allowed myself to become. I have become apathetic to continually learning. That seriously needs to change; never again will I allow apathy to distract me from devoting some consistent measure of time to continually improving, refining, or otherwise enhancing my business knowledge. Easier said than done. Where should I start? I sighed heavily and thought, *Now that's a perplexing question.*

Start at the beginning seems like the obvious answer. My inner Yoda calmly states, "Start at the beginning, you must." HA! I am 100% a product of my generation. Oh well, it is time to go home; I can't solve all the challenges of my life in a single day.

BEYOND THE SMILE

*Every part of an interaction with
another party is selling.*

Today is going to be a great day, or not. A dentist's appointment at 8:15 AM. What had I been thinking when agreeing to an early appointment that was offered to me six months ago during my regular cleaning visit? As I wheeled around the parking lot looking for a convenient parking space, my thoughts went to the friendly staff at Cassie's office. The employees made me feel less nervous when I visited their office. My fear of visiting medical care professionals of any kind was something that defied explanation; since my youth, visiting the dentist was never what one might describe as a calm or joyous experience. My apprehension was always high before visiting the office; my blood pressure ran high during the appointment. Over the years, each of our family moves has required us to find new healthcare professionals. Our move a few years ago led us to discover Cassie. My wife searched online for reviews and found someone great with kids, specializing in family care dentistry. Secretly, I think that's the code for when there's an overgrown baby in the family, we can take care of them *too*!

Yes, that's me, and I am thankful for my wife's sensitivity about my nervous nature when it comes to having someone do things to my teeth. Apparently, I'm not alone in the world regarding dental apprehension; dentists prescribe medication and offer sedation treatments for cleanings. At least I'm not so afraid that drugs are needed for a routine visit.

As I walked into the building and waited for the elevator to reach the first floor for my ride upstairs, my apprehension rose. Stepping into the elevator meant being halfway from the parking lot to the office entrance. *Maybe I should reschedule. Do I need to go to the dentist today? Yes. Yes, I do.* The doors opened, and I looked down at the tile floor; *one step forward is all it takes to get moving.* Willing myself forward from the elevator, I entered Cassie's office and surrendered myself to the process.

The receptionist smiled and said, "Welcome to our office. Thanks for coming in today. How may I help you?" There is just something about a warm smile that diffuses tension. This was a prime example of the right person in the right position treating a customer the right way.

Already feeling more at ease, I said, "Hi. I'm Sam, and my appointment is at 8:15."

She smiled again, "Hi Sam. We've been expecting you. Thanks for confirming your appointment online." She passed me an iPad, "We have a couple of documents for your review; after you look to make sure your information is still correct, you can sign and return the tablet to me. May I get you anything while you're waiting? We have water and some other assorted refreshments if you're thirsty."

"No, thank you. I'm ok for now."

With another pleasant smile, she said, "Let me know if you change your mind. If you would like, you're welcome to take a seat for a minute or two until your hygienist calls you back. Let me know if you have questions about your forms or need help with anything."

My apprehension continued as I checked a few boxes and signed disclosures. I swiftly confirmed some things, returned the iPad, and resumed my seat. After just a few minutes, my hygienist invited me back to begin my visit. Everything went smoothly for the rest of the appointment, so I needn't have worried.

When I left Cassie's office, my thoughts turned to how efficient the experience had been for me and the many other patients I had spotted during my visit. I need to sit down for a few minutes and process my interaction. There are some lessons to be learned from my visit. There is a great coffee shop nearby; I started the short walk as I began reflecting.

I doubt that my company makes each interaction as painless and smooth as the experience a customer has when entering the engagement with a high level of apprehension. We don't drill people's teeth for fillings or perform root canals, yet I wonder how many people leave our business smiling or at least feeling more at ease about their situation?

I lost myself in the process of ordering and receiving a black-eye coffee, pouring just the perfect amount of half-and-half, and adding a little sweetener to make the perfect cup of brew. The smoothness of an efficient customer experience was apparent. It was similar yet different from my dentist visit. Well, now that I think about it, maybe a pleasurable exchange of a product or service for compensation has few differences beyond the name of what is being traded.

After finding a seat in one of the coffee shop's corners, I continued thinking about how the dentist visit was managed. What made my visit stand out from the average? Was it just the smile offered in greeting by the person at the front desk when I entered the office, or something more?

After a warm greeting, and only waiting a few minutes after filling out my paperwork, the hygienist's warm greeting was the next notable event. Not only was he friendly and smiling when he welcomed me back, but it was also noticeable that the office was prepared to receive me as a patient. That made me feel valued as a customer. My time is just as important as that of a dentist, doctor, attorney, accountant, or other service professional in any industry; the hourly or visit rate is irrelevant.

My time is precious to me; it is my own. How would anyone know the value of my time versus another person's time? What if my time at an appointment was longer than expected, cutting into time with a sick relative or causing me to be late for my kid's play at school? That is a key thought and something that has always bothered me about different professions and my interaction with companies over the years. Every time I visit the doctor, I always have the same thoughts.

Waiting in a doctor's office for thirty or forty minutes is preposterous. The amount of money being charged or earned by someone is irrelevant to the customer. The patient's time is more critical to the patient than the doctor's time is to the patient. That is the core concept; it is not about the doctor, it is about the patient. Respecting my time, Cassie's office made me feel respected. That made a tremendous difference in my day. That little thing that is not so little is essential. *A service or goods provider should consider the customer's time*; that is a key concept. Cassie has that part of her company functioning at an elevated level, and it is not by accident.

When my hygienist performed the cleaning, he efficiently did his work while engaging me in just enough conversation to convey that he cared about what was happening in my day. My comfort mattered. He was pretty smooth in the conversational exchange, asking just the correct number of questions about flossing, brushing, or any discomfort experienced to gather what he needed for the charts. He did all of that while keeping my mind on the other parts of our little chat. He would make a great salesperson. Would make? He is a great salesperson! He is selling a process or interaction; it just happens to involve oral health care. Another key thought is that *every part of an interaction with another party is a form of selling*.

During Cassie's visit, she performed an examination, asking about my family and work, and quickly reviewed my cleaning notes on the monitor. After examining me, she declared my oral health to be excellent and asked if I had any questions. She even asked how their new system for appointment confirmation was working, inquiring further whether the text and email were sufficient as reminders or if a call was preferred. I thought little of it during the visit, but her concern was for the entire process, not just the actual exam. Another key concept was revealed. *Concern for a customer involves every part of the experience; what happens before, during, and after an exchange matters.*

I sat in the coffee shop for a while observing the exchange between baristas and customers; each one a little different, each one essentially alike. The customer placed an order, the barista prepared it, the customer picked up their brew, and moved forward in life; a life made just a little better by something as simple as a caffeine-laden, syrup-flavored liquid. Customers often ordered simple coffee, as I preferred, but more seemed to enjoy slight variations of the more flavored concoctions offered on the menu. Either way, the exchange was pleasant with the barista always encouraging the customer to let them know if the drink was satisfactory or if anything could be done to improve the taste. The recipes seemed to be the same, yet taste buds varied. It was catering to the particular tastes of each customer on every drink that spoke volumes of the dedication to the entire customer experience. *Equally crucial to the efficient delivery of goods and services is providing customers with precisely what they want, in the way they want it.*

I walked across the common area of the market center towards my car. As I enjoyed my coffee, absorbing the surrounding business interactions, the realization dawned on me: every business interaction teaches something about good or bad customer experiences. Many people will do business with individuals or companies they do not find attractive if the business or person is meeting the customer's dominant need. Great businesses motivate people to shop with the company multiple times. *Each interaction matters; performing well, and more importantly, more often than the competition, results in a higher lifetime value of a customer.*

REWRITE THE STORY

*Opportunity is neither given nor automatic;
it is created.*

The grass was freshly trimmed, rows of white chairs were carefully arranged to allow at least a thousand attendees to sit with a view of the stage, yellow and black ribbons adorned chairs on the end of the rows, and the excitement of families chattering about how their son, daughter, brother, sister, or in-law would launch into an exciting career in the law permeated the already-humid air of Houston in May.

Ariel was the youngest of three children and the first to graduate from law school. The older siblings chose medicine; it seemed normal and almost expected, considering her father, a dentist, and her mother, a pediatrician, had dedicated their lives to serving the health needs of others. It was easy to follow in the footsteps of parents who had already blazed a trail; the health-related vocabulary of children raised in such a household surpasses that of the average EMT or Dental Hygienist before the child graduates from high school.

It was assumed that Ariel would follow a similar path into a field related to healthcare. Everyone thought this would be the case until the fall of her senior year in college, when Ariel announced during Thanksgiving dinner that she planned to apply to law school. The silence at the table was deafening for about twenty seconds until Grandpa chimed in and said, "I thought you might do something a little different with your life. I have been wondering for a while where you would land, and now, I know. Good for you, sweetie; I am certain your reputation as a brilliant lawyer will be known amongst your peers."

With that proclamation from the honor seat of the table, the potential critics were forever silenced, and Ariel beamed with pride every time she talked about law school. Her enthusiasm was infectious, and a family of people dedicated to health care became fans of the law. The discussions during family gatherings had a new flavor as Ariel progressed from a 1L to a 2L and finally a 3L student. I was unsure if a group of people could possibly be prouder of a family member until I looked around at the hundreds of faces proudly watching the stage when we attended Ariel's graduation.

My sister-in-law appeared extremely excited. It was a day that would forever be remembered as a moment when hard work and dedication were recognized. It suited her personality well to be the center of attention in a family of overachievers. The youngest, the different one, never a conformist, she beamed radiantly in the spotlight. It was fitting that she would forge her path and pursue her passion purposefully.

Like Grampa, I assumed from the very first time we met that she would do something different with her life. Perhaps that is why we connected so easily, and our discussions over the years flowed naturally. It was not just because she was the youngest sibling of the woman I loved; it was a connection related to some part of our personalities that made me a poor employee and a great salesperson at the same time. Her fearless nature could make her a natural salesperson. Being a prominent lawyer seems to involve sales within the legal profession. Lawyers must either excel at securing clients or work with firms that are skilled at securing clients; either way, someone has to secure the job before anyone else can do the job. I respected her willingness to go against conforming opinions and blaze her own trail in law school.

She had often asked me what it was like to be in sales. Those questions usually prompted discussions related to being fearless in business, not taking no for an answer until it was given at least ten times, and thinking outside the box to accomplish tasks that seemed impossible to those less dedicated or mentally equipped to succeed in sales.

The thoughts of many discussions on her parents' patio during holidays and family visits drifted through my memory as I waited for the ceremony to begin. A smile formed as I thought about how brave she was to venture into a new field. It was the same type of bravery I respected in my wife, who chose to work in the health clinic for half of each workweek to support the community. The sacrifice in pay was a wonderful exchange for the increased self-worth she felt for delivering excellent care to those unable to afford traditional health services. Sacrificing something to accomplish what you believe should be done, or doing something you can when many are unwilling, shows character. To me, that is heroic.

The pageantry of the day was infectious; it seemed only natural that every aspect induced thoughts of the future. Hopes and dreams seemed vibrantly displayed on the face of every graduate. It had been a while since I had experienced an event serving as the celebration of finishing something that would catalyze future careers and lives. Maybe I'm getting sentimental; the ceremony seems to be as much about the future as the past.

Maybe there is wisdom in that thought; *use the past as a foundation upon which to build the future.* Perhaps I could be more heroic in my life. The world could use a few more heroes. Internally smirking, I wonder what sort of insurance guy could be a hero?

Roll cameras; introducing this year's hero of the year for our town, Sam the insurance guy!

Okay, insurance may not land me on the nightly news as the local hero of the week; perhaps insurance could be the vehicle of heroic action that serves the community. Nightly news or not, some heroes are people who quietly make a difference, and I would like that to be part of my future. Now that is a thought to ponder.

How can my company be a community hero? What can we offer to support and enrich the lives of those in the town? Be the hero in my own story; now that is a worthy goal.

Not all life's challenges can be solved in a day; this requires more thought. I want my life's work to be about more than the money I make for myself and my family. I want to derive feelings of accomplishment for doing something that is more, different, or better for those in my community. I could have sold equipment forever; I must consider the insurance company a vehicle of opportunity.

Talking to several of Ariel's friends during the past three years revealed to me that while money motivates some, it's not the primary driver for most. Many of her friends consider themselves defenders of the innocent and advocates for the law. Their youthful optimism about the world sometimes felt naïve, yet their resolve to change it remained unshaken. I developed a newfound opinion of lawyers from those interactions. After all, don't we all want a better future for those we love and care about? It seems natural to hope for something better, especially if you're willing to sacrifice to bring about something better for yourself and those you love. In the end, isn't that what going to school is about, hoping for something better in the future by sacrificing time for the duration of the educational program?

Almost as if on cue, my thoughts were brought back to my present surroundings as the music started playing to signify the beginning of the graduation procession. Classical music, setting an official yet uplifting tone, drifted through the air as the announcer called out the professors' names. After they reached the middle of the stage, the announcer named the graduates individually as they crossed the stage. After the announcer named everyone, the crowd rose and applauded the graduating class. Cameras flashed to memorialize the moment of sons and daughters making the ceremonial graduation march; nods of approval were shared between parent and child, siblings, and best friends; tears of pride and joy were dabbed from smiling faces as several hundred graduates made their way to their appointed seats in front of the elevated stage area. Three trumpeters signaled the crowd to quiet and focus attention on the front stage.

The entire event, which lasted a couple of hours, went smoothly; several professors, the class president, and the class valedictorian delivered speeches. While the past three years were touched upon, most speakers dedicated more time to discussing their future hopes and dreams. Advice on shaping the future into what you want it to be, reminders to hold on to the passion for the law, and encouragement to trust in that same passion when times become tough were dominant themes among the speakers.

For many years, Ariel seemed to view me as a mentor, or maybe the big brother she had never had. Regardless, she often sought advice or shared thoughts while grappling with a puzzling situation. Unsurprisingly, she sought me out when we arrived back at her parents' home to continue the celebration. Because the day was so inviting, I had opted to enjoy the fresh air on the patio. Ariel joined me for a glass of champagne to discuss her thoughts about her future after law school.

"I just don't understand," she exclaimed. "I worked my butt off while attending law school and the only job offers I got were to practice in the District Attorney's office or join a firm as a clerk. Are you kidding me?! I invested over $200,000 to attend law school; the thought of taking a job that pays $50,000 a year is off the table. Maybe I should have gone into medicine; school would have been easier, and I would already be placed in a hospital."

She sounded so defeated. Her body language and tonal inflections showed an elevated level of frustration and anxiety; it certainly seemed at odds with the rest of the day's celebrations and positivity.

Sensing a teachable moment was presenting itself, I smiled a little, thinking that I want more of helping someone grow personally or professionally to be part of my life. "Tell me about what's on your mind. What has you so out of sorts?"

She sighed heavily and said, "Getting a job."

"Your tone doesn't sound like the girl who broke family tradition to attend law school," I offered.

"The girl who attended law school didn't have the same realization that competition would be so fierce in the job market."

Her frustration seemed unusually intense, especially considering it was only hours post-graduation. I knew that the bar exam was still months away. A little confused, but wanting to help, I asked, "Tell me about getting a job. What has you focused on employment right now?"

Ariel sighed heavily again before beginning her explanation. "Each student in the class is ranked against all other students in the graduating class. Class ranking is often considered the most important factor in securing a job interview. Essentially, if you are not in the top ten percent of your class, interviews with top firms in the area are never offered. Getting an interview does not automatically equal getting the job, yet never getting an interview makes it virtually impossible. Most graduates who get interviews get offers from one or several of the firms interviewing those candidates. Those interviews have been happening throughout the last semester."

I was beginning to understand the situation, but I wanted her to figure out the solution herself, so I asked, "Aren't you graduating with honors? Isn't that enough to get the attention of potential employers?"

With another heavy sigh, as if burdened by the world, she continued, "Yes, but not the right employers. At least not the kind of employers that pay well and offer associate positions. To answer the other question, I am graduating with honors. Even though I graduated with a very respectable ranking, I still wasn't among the top tier of graduates. Sadly, my first semester of law school was my worst, and the grades weighed down my grade point average just enough to keep me out of the top group. That is the source of my frustration. I'm graduating from an excellent law school, with honors, and am struggling to land a job. How broken is the system?"

Barely taking a breath, she conveyed more of her thoughts, "One of my classmates is so desperate, she is taking a job as a paralegal. A paralegal. Are. You. Kidding. Me? You can get that job after a few classes at the local community college; ok, more than just a few classes, but you understand what I mean. On a serious note, I didn't study the law for three years to do a job I don't need a law degree to perform. That is just silly."

Sensing this might be a suitable time to offer a little more straightforward advice, I said, "Let's talk a little more about the challenges you're facing in the job market. Ultimately, that's the actual issue. Ranking in the top ten percent often results in excellent job offers. Ranking in the bottom ninety percent still results in earning a law degree?"

She nodded, and I continued, "And, as you, like all your classmates, will be issued law degrees, you're entitled to take the Bar exam. Correct?" She nodded again. "So, what you're telling me is that you're going to graduate from a great school with a law degree and may take the exam that, assuming you pass and I'm sure you will, results in being licensed to practice law in the state of Texas."

She said, "All of that is true, and I think I see where you're going with this line of thought."

I leaned a little forward while looking directly into her eyes and, with one eyebrow slightly raised, said, "I'm sure you do; just to be sure, share your thoughts. Where do you think I'm going in the conversation?"

She offered the slightest sigh and said, "OK, OK, you win. I get it. My opportunities are still there. Just because I didn't get a fantastic job offer before graduation doesn't mean I don't have opportunities."

I looked at her for a moment and said, "And?"

A self-resigned, optimistic smile touched her lips. "And opportunities are there for the taking. I need to create those opportunities. I need to stop worrying about what I don't have or what someone else has and concentrate on what advantages are available to me. I have been so self-absorbed and feeling sorry for myself that I overlooked the obvious. Just because something isn't handed to me on a silver platter doesn't mean it is out of reach if effort is applied to accomplish a goal or objective."

"Welcome to the real world," I offered with a smile. "Contrary to what is conveyed via marketing by universities and promised during political elections, if you want something better or more than what you have now, you need to be prepared to pursue your goals with little help from the system. Universities are businesses in the field of education; rarely, if ever, in the bold or fine print of educational marketing will you ever find language conveying a guarantee of employment upon graduation. An education can help, it never hurts, but it does not create entitlement. Politicians often proclaim things like "healthcare for all" and "education for all," among others. Those things, so easily promised from a podium, come with a cost. The burden of the expense is shouldered by those who are listening, not those making the promises. To think otherwise is naïve."

I continued, "That view is not meant to be cynical or harsh, but I'm sharing it so you're not surprised in the future. Graduating from law school is not an automatic winning lottery ticket to life; it is more like an opportunity you use to make or create other opportunities for yourself in life. Make sense?"

She looked at me with a newfound understanding of the world's rules and said, "I understand. What you're saying seems logical. I know you, and many others in my life, have shared the same or similar thoughts with me before today; it just didn't mean as much until now. When the student is ready, the teacher appears, I suppose."

We wrapped up the conversation, and during the following months, Ariel showed she understood. She began networking with attorneys in Houston through social events, submitting her resume for consideration, and interacting with professors to secure referrals for job leads. When she took the Bar exam in August, she had already interviewed with several firms and received two exciting job offers. The best part of that process was how proud she felt about creating the opportunity. During those same summer months, I continued to ponder my situation with the office to gain insight into solutions to my professional challenges.

Spotting solutions for others when examining a personal or work situation can be easy when there is no emotional attachment to the people or situation; what is obvious to someone on the outside isn't always so apparent to those experiencing the event or series of events. Life is messy and emotional, especially when discussing your own life.

Opportunity is neither given nor automatic; it is created. The challenge of creating opportunities in small businesses may be straightforward or complex, effortless or difficult to discover and implement; the only certainty is that we are self-empowered to find enlightenment through our thoughts or by seeking the counsel of others. Improvement is possible with a plan.

BETWEEN JOB AND DREAMS

Sometimes the hardest part of moving forward is admitting the old path no longer serves you.

The spectacular view of one of Charleston's many harbors was visible while sitting on the hotel's top-floor lounge balcony. The view across Lockwood Drive seemed exceptionally breathtaking in the early morning hours. The coffee was fresh, the breeze gently blowing, and anticipating the forthcoming conversation was enough to put a genuine, ear-to-ear smile on my face. While traveling on business, a networking app alert on my phone led to a meeting with my friend, Julian. He had just left his previous employer to start an accounting firm; the job change of a first-tier contact resulted in an alert. Having recently departed the corporate world, I pondered his adjustment and subsequently sent a congratulatory email along with an invitation to meet when I next visit the area.

He responded enthusiastically about the meeting and pointed out that we have both been lax over the last ten years on staying in touch. The resulting emails and texts had us bantering back and forth, just as we did in college. Julian, easily one of the most optimistic students in several of my classes, had always been quick to make friends and contacts. It was easy to fall back into the straightforward exchange typical of our college days. I wonder what Julian might share today about starting his firm.

There it is; Julian's text letting me know he needed entry to the lounge. I walked across the concierge lounge to meet him at the door. "Hi Sam. It is terrific to see you."

"It is great to see you too, Julian. I've been looking forward to seeing you in person. You look fantastic. Work and family life seem to agree with you."

We shook hands and embraced each other with a quick hug as a greeting. I motioned in a welcoming way towards the interior of the lounge. "Come in, come in. I've got seats for us on the balcony. Each one is semiprivate; I thought it might be a better place for us to chat. As a bonus, the view is exceptional."

He nodded in agreement. "That sounds perfect. Should we grab a little food and coffee to take with us?"

"Of course, that's a plan that works for me."

After making our way to the table, Julian said, "I have been through some challenges lately, and I'm eager to share. Before we get to that, how is the family? Everyone doing great, kids, wife? Happy wife, happy life."

With a slight chuckle, "Yes. Things are fantastic at home right now. The kids are doing great, and my wife is happy. She loves her job and is extremely supportive of my work. If anything, she has more faith in me than ever. You?"

Julian responded, "Things are going well in my personal life. My wife stopped working to care for our boys when we found out we had a girl on the way."

"Wow, congratulations, Julian!"

A smile accompanied his words. "Thanks, Sam. I appreciate you saying that. As you are aware from my profile and our previous emails, I transitioned from working in the finance department at the auto plant to opening my own office. I'm operating solo and developing a business by helping small business owners prioritize ROI and manage cash flow. There seems to be a lack of people servicing small businesses, and I'm hoping to fill in the gap."

"That is not exactly what I expected when I learned you ventured to start a company independently. I thought you may have secured a contract with one of the local manufacturing companies for some special projects or consulting work. Based on the last ten or more years you have been doing manufacturing-related accounting services, I thought you would be a natural to do that kind of work. You're totally switching gears," I stated.

Julian then offered a slight smile before he replied. Something seemed a little *off* to me. There was just a little catch in his tone. "Yes. That is spot on. I'm shifting the area of focus from manufacturing to something else entirely. I grew tired of the grind-it-out hours, receiving little recognition, only to be rewarded with moderate pay raises at the end of each year. I could work forty hours or eighty hours a week, my volume of work could be low or high; no one seemed to notice. If they noticed, they barely acknowledged it and never rewarded me. I grew tired of the politics and of answering to people content to hold a spot until a distant retirement."

A slight frown touched his face. "My apologies. That was less than gracious. A fairer description of what bothered me was that people above me planned to stay in place for the next fifteen or twenty years. They are all older than I; most are the age I hope to be when I retire. Instead of retirement, most have shared their intent to work for as long as they are contractually allowed; further, they frequently made such comments in front of everyone in the department. Their seemingly continual oratory on work catalyzed thoughts related to the next ten years of my life. I realized my work earned me nothing except the right to wait in line for another fifteen or twenty. That was unacceptable."

I sipped my coffee and paused before I responded. Julian seemed pretty bothered after sharing some of his story. "That is an earful. And, I'm sorry to hear about your unpleasant experience."

Julian leaned back in his chair. He was less animated and excited as he took a few breaths. "I guess I was holding back a little in my emails. I have always felt so at ease with you, Sam. I suppose I needed to purge. I'm still wrapping my mind around my frustration, and it's a little tough to think about how my career stalled."

He continued, "Now that I'm listening to myself say this out loud, it occurs to me the decision to forge my path and open my company had more to do with those feelings than a burning desire to build a business. I just wanted to be appreciated; instead, I faced fifteen more years of grind. It occurred to me that I had overestimated my importance to the company. When I joined the team, I thought I would be the Chief Financial Officer in ten years; sadly, the realization of my role is now crystal clear. I was just another cog in the wheel."

This conversation has taken a more serious turn than I expected. Rather than a triumphant tale of launching his firm, Julian's story is overshadowed by lingering resentment from his previous job. I nodded sympathetically and said, "Julian, I understand. I do. That isn't what I expected to hear this morning, but it isn't too far off the mark from my situation. Although the circumstances regarding my decision to work with my father for a brief period while he transitioned his ownership shares to me were a little different, some of what you experienced are things I can relate to with my previous job."

Julian looked at me pleadingly. "Would you mind sharing? Strangely, I feel a little better knowing I'm not alone in my feelings."

My emotional state was seemingly far beyond Julian's, so I had no problem disclosing some information. "Absolutely. I believe our situations are quite common. I received excellent treatment and fair compensation by any standard. It was a job, not a career; there is a difference. If I needed any proof to convince myself this was the case, I found it a few days after leaving. When I dropped by my old office to pick up a few remaining personal items, I discovered that my replacement was already working my old accounts. I don't think orders slowed down one bit. I could have worked there through retirement. Had I stayed for ten more years, I would likely have been promoted to sales management or vice president. The ten-year discussion happened with my division leader just a few weeks before I visited with Dad. Obviously, you know the choice I made."

Julian nodded. "I knew you left. I heard about it from Jimmy. We stayed in touch after meeting at your cousin's wedding. I think that guy could befriend a porcupine."

We both laughed, understanding each other's appreciation for how Jimmy never met a stranger; the word 'stranger' did not apply after the first few minutes of meeting. Jimmy was a natural salesperson.

Julian continued, "He has been a real inspiration to me in starting my office. I mentioned it to him after seeing one of his posts on social media. I responded and mentioned the possibility of starting a company; the rest is history. His enthusiasm is infectious."

I replied, "That much is true. Tell me about what has been happening with your office. You've been at it for a few months now. What's happening with getting customers?"

Julian looked sheepishly at me and said, "I barely have any clients. The ones I'm talking to haven't contracted me to do work, so I guess you could say my current position is a prospecting professional. Sam, I feel terrible even sharing these things. I always thought of you as a good friend. Although we live in different cities and aren't as close as we used to be, you were always someone I felt comfortable confiding in back in college. I guess my feelings in that department never changed. That being said, I intended to come here this morning to put on a brave face and keep the conversation light; I didn't think our talk could get so heavy and certainly not before finishing our food and first cup of brew. I'm making a mess of this meeting."

Because I sensed his obvious concern, I said, "Julian, you never need to pretend with me. Save that for people you don't know. If you are high or low, you're still a friend. I'd rather have the real Julian than a made-up version, intending to smooth over a breakfast meeting. Instead of worrying about what I think, or might think about your situation, why don't we put our heads together like we did back in school and come up with a game plan to move you forward in your business? Truthfully, it will help me too. We haven't delved into my situation, but I'm struggling with a few challenges myself. I've exchanged one job for another. The potential is there for me to change it, yet I'm puzzled about how to turn that into my reality. What do you say?"

Julian visibly relaxed and said, "I don't have anyone to talk to because everyone I know here is associated with my old job or a friend. Those friends could be more accurately labeled as acquaintances, and I don't want to share my worries or concerns with anyone in our social circle. I'm too worried they will judge me or, worse yet, say something that will hurt my chances of success with the new endeavor."

I felt compelled to help as best as possible and said, "Let's make beneficial use of our time and dive right into our challenges. Tell me about what is happening with your business."

Julian nodded as he leaned in a little to share his story. "As I have already shared the frustrations with the job, I will spare us both any more details. That is ancient history. My primary aim is to move my business forward. I need to generate some clients and some revenue."

"Tell me about the clients you're working to get. What sort of businesses or customers are you trying to service?" I asked.

Julian continued, "I left and thought I might pursue contracts with businesses experiencing cash flow challenges. You know, these situations often involve owing money to suppliers or collecting accounts receivable. Reworking their pay schedule or helping to negotiate a payment schedule for outstanding monies could be of significant benefit to a client. My thought was that the idea was sound and the service useful. My expectations were perhaps a little higher than what has become my reality."

He slowly shook his head resignedly and said, "I've only signed a few clients, despite over forty meetings and countless calls. I'm contacting lawyers and large accounting firms serving business owners; a few have sent potential customers. At first, things seemed to go great. At least, that is what I thought when people started getting in touch via phone or email about a meeting. Unfortunately, those referred weren't referred without cause. I didn't expect that the companies sending me business would only refer clients who could not pay their fees."

I figured that would be a tricky situation. Julian's situation seemed to be bleak. "Well, if your firm is chosen by referring professionals for work they consider unprofitable or difficult to bill, then it sounds quite challenging."

Julian then revealed more details that confirmed my fears for him and caused even more concern. "The people who get in touch typically can't afford a retainer. Several attempted to negotiate my fee to less than $500 for the entire engagement. My business plan projections were built around five thousand dollars, or more, annual revenue per client."

Wondering if he was already working on securing other types of clients, I asked, "So what have you done? Are you going to keep going down this path or change direction?"

He smiled resignedly and admitted, "Very little, other than that very question, has been on my mind over the last several days. My last meeting on Thursday morning was the proverbial straw that broke the camel's back. After being asked to do the work for free, in exchange for future opportunities to do annual tax returns for the company, I realized that something had to change."

Frustration, clearly, influenced his decision-making. "Ok," I prompted, aiming to stimulate more discussion and contemplation. "Let's assume your prior experiences are the norm. What can you do differently to get a customer, or more accurately, customers plural, that will pay fees aligned with your expectations? Or, if you cannot secure customers willing to pay, what new types of customers will you try to get?"

Julian said, "I'm currently marketing to get customers or clients not represented by an accountant or attorney, but that effort will probably be a slow process. I have a website designed to capture leads from people with challenges. I've only garnered a few leads from the site."

His prospecting sparked my interest; I inquired about the quantity and quality of his leads.

A tight smile, almost a grimace, hinted at his resignation as he explained, "Many of my site's visitors appear to have already researched extensively on other websites and blogs. As a result, they're adept at finding solutions to challenges. To be honest, my advice is quite simple. My true value lies in being a local expert who provides qualified advice, coaching, and encouragement to help businesspeople make informed decisions and follow through on them. In recent years, social media advice has become increasingly helpful in assisting people in tackling their problems. Nevertheless, many still struggle."

Julian continued, "There appear to be some dominant reasons many fail after implementing their own solutions. First, many seem to fail because of the lack of follow-through on a decision; old habits sometimes die hard. Second, others fail because the advice they are taking is from someone great at promotion on social media, but lacks any depth of understanding in business. Finally, others fail because the advice given is brilliant for maybe 90% of all businesses. Still, it isn't the right advice for the circumstances of the person receiving and acting upon that advice. In short, most people don't feel they need a professional, even if they really do."

Seeming to have a moment of clarity and realization, he uttered, "Too bad I didn't figure this out until after launching the business."

Julian, no longer offering even a forced smile, frowned and looked downward while shaking his head. "Honestly, Sam, I wasted a lot of valuable time. Time I don't have because I'm living off quickly dwindling savings. I have about twelve weeks to generate revenue or phase out of this type of work. Phasing out means getting a new job. This just got seriously heavy. I haven't even admitted that to myself, much less to my wife or anyone else. The thought just struck me, this company may not survive."

After hearing Julian's candid assessment, I agreed with it. I said, "Tell me what you think you might do if this doesn't work. What is Plan B? Do you have a Plan B?"

ALWAYS HAVE A PLAN B

Realizing where you stand is the first step to deciding where you want to go.

Julian seemed particularly troubled as he uttered, "You know, Sam, until this morning I thought I had a plan A. Right now, I don't think I have a solid plan A, much less a Plan B."

I declared, "Easy. Don't let things get away from you emotionally. I know it is not just business, it is personal. It is your life we're talking about here. That being said, realizing where you stand is a good first step in figuring out where you want to go."

Julian replied, "Ok. I admit it, I'm feeling uneasy about where things stand with my company right now. As I mentioned, I haven't thought about it like this until now. I need a new plan."

With relief, I nodded. "That sounds more like the Julian I know. Let's talk about your plan to make things better. If you accomplish nothing else today other than come up with changed or revised primary and contingent plans, you will be in a much better position to move forward. Agreed?"

He nodded and said, "Sorry to rehash, but it may help me to summarize where I stand right now. Stop me if you feel like I'm getting off track. Apparently, purging thoughts with you helps me see things more clearly. I guess that's called saying the quiet part out loud. Sometimes that can be a good thing."

He continued, "My current situation is that after pursuing clients with cash challenges for the past couple of months, results have been less than desired. Clients are more limited in terms of availability than I expected. Further complicating the lack of candidates is the limited number of companies with enough additional cash flow or capital to pay my fees. My original business plan appears to be limited in scope due to these unforeseen facts regarding revenue generation. I need to pivot, generate some revenue fast, or else develop an exit strategy."

I interjected, "Exit strategy?"

Julian nodded, "Yes. It seems evident to me, as of today, that I need to consider seeking other opportunities if this company doesn't move forward soon. I believe this needs to be my Plan B. With limited reserve capital and cash flow, my efforts can realistically continue for another three months. I could stretch for another thirty days after that, but that would be tough on the family."

"I recently heard from a consultant I met that part of planning to take action is setting specific goals. So, tell me about the next ninety days." I looked intently at Julian and hoped he might have some good thoughts about moving his business in a better direction.

With something like a resigned look on his face, Julian continued his brainstorming, "First things first. I should probably seek traditional clients. I could do tax work, or perhaps seek small subcontractor suppliers for local plants that need accounting assistance. This could be my entry point into a relationship. I began my career working with numerous small business owners, providing basic bookkeeping services. There isn't much money in the day-to-day services, but this would provide two things: cash flow and potential work. This is essentially building a traditional practice. I must admit, I'm not too excited about building a traditional practice, even though it could work. My early years entailed a lot of this type of work, and this feels a little like going backwards. I need a minute to think this through a little more."

He continued, "Starting a new company without something that differentiates me from my competition would make for a rough re-launch of the business. Not that my efforts to date have produced much of a launch."

"Don't be so hard on yourself."

Julian shrugged. "It is what it is. There is no need to sugar-coat the truth. I acted out of frustration with my previous job and seized upon what I thought was a wonderful concept. In reality, I didn't spend enough time examining the market for available clients, competitive pressure, or exploitable advantage. My jump into launching a company was about as graceful as a cat trying to swim laps in a swimming pool." He laughed at his situation resignedly, then a smile showed that something like relief crossed his face.

"Julian, you ok?"

"Yeah, I'm good, or at least I think I will be soon. I need to give this situation some thought. Regardless of where things lead, I want to put more effort into planning for round two than I did for my initial launch. I suppose the question of the day is, what do I want to do with the rest of my life? Whatever choices I make now will impact my professional and personal happiness for many years to come. Although I feel a little foolish reflecting on my current status and the poor initial decisions I've made, life is about learning from mistakes. This one seems like it may be costly; all the more reason to learn the lesson well and not repeat the error."

I replied, "I know what you mean about making a few challenging decisions. As I mentioned earlier, my current situation could best be described as a job. I am a part-owner of the company, with no plans to transition from working as a valued employee to becoming a full-fledged business owner. On the surface, some people might think they are the same. Yet, I feel as though, unless the enterprise can sustain itself without my continual injection of capital through my sales, it is merely a place I work with my name on some ownership documents. I suppose passing it to my kids, like my father did to me, could be a good thing. If that is the only upside, I want other options."

Julian said, "I understand that motivation. I knew that, upon entering my current situation, I would have a job for a while, with 'a while' being defined as a few years at most, before expanding to include other associates. I had not thought beyond that point about getting out of doing the day-to-day work and replicating my efforts through others. That vaguely feels like some management definition: replication of effort via leading others to do more than you can do on your own. Is that how you think?"

I responded, "Right now, I'm the only person selling, or at least trying to sell new accounts. My partner is maintaining accounts gained over the years; there is no actual plan to transition those clients to me or another person. Furthermore, if he were no longer in the picture because of his choices or extenuating circumstances, there is no guarantee the company would retain those relationships. I'm spending most of my time servicing the clients my father acquired over the years, and any extra time available, I'm attempting to increase the book of business. Understandably, he is doing much of the same work I'm doing now. At first, I didn't understand the amount of effort that would take; now I have a firmer grasp of what it means to maintain a book of business."

I continued, "Knowing that I'll eventually cap out the number of newly generated accounts versus my ability to service new and existing customers, I have been thinking about bringing additional salespeople aboard; my thoughts have not resulted in many actions. Or perhaps bringing additional support staff on board. Something. Regardless, you have the excuse of just getting started. I lack the same excuse as I bought into an existing operation."

Julian replied, "I can see you're a little frustrated. We seem to both be at a point where we need a better plan. We need a vision for what we want our respective companies to look like in one year or, more importantly, in five years."

I responded, "I agree one hundred percent. The thought of waking up in five years and having the same challenges does not seem the least bit appealing. I'm unsure what I want it to be, but I know I don't want to stand still for five or more years. If I were going to do that, I could have continued logging hours at my old job. I want to be a business owner. That much I know."

Having become conscious of the time spent in conversation, I needed to wrap things up… at least for now. "What does your afternoon look like? I have a meeting in about an hour; my presentation requires a little last-minute preparation to shine. I can't afford to misfire on this one, but would love to get together later today if you're available to continue the discussion."

Julian responded, "That sounds great. I need a little time to digest what we discussed. My schedule is pretty flexible today; the freedom usually feels overwhelming, but today it feels liberating, as I'm able to use it to plan for a better future. How does 2:30 sound?"

"Perfect. I'll see you back here at the hotel?"

Julian nodded in the affirmative. "See you after lunch."

As Julian left the lounge, I moved back to my seat on the balcony to make a few tweaks to the PowerPoint for the meeting later in the morning. Making a few changes made me feel as though the presentation gained ready status, and I sat back to enjoy a few more minutes of contemplation before the Uber arrived to take me to the client meeting.

Reflecting on this morning's exchange, I gained clarity on some specific aspects of my company. Julian's situation allowed me to focus on my professional challenges.

First, I felt encouraged that I wasn't alone in my struggle. My feelings towards Julian did not incline towards wanting him to feel stressed; the opposite of stressed would more accurately describe my wishes for him. Julian is an intelligent person; business solutions are not always easy to see, especially when you're in the business, trying to solve challenges you're emotionally attached to in your company or business endeavors. Ownership isn't as easy as it looks on the surface.

Second, I have developed a newfound respect for my partner and my father; I'm sure they faced some of these same types of challenges within the company. How to grow while simultaneously managing current clients isn't as simple as it looks from the outside. Their efforts and hard work led to their present situation, avoiding a potentially worse one. The insurance industry, particularly the commercial insurance sector, is highly competitive.

Finally, I don't want to make mistakes and endanger what my father helped create, but moving the company forward to become a proper business is my goal. I'm sure it won't be easy; I'm pretty convinced it's possible. Maintaining the status quo is not my highest aspiration; I changed from industrial sales to build something greater for me and my family.

All of those thoughts are good in that I have some sense of what I want and do not want; that doesn't specifically describe what I want the business to become. What is my vision? What are my goals beyond being knee deep in this situation and wanting to avoid failure? Are vision and goals the same thing? This feels like some hefty mental lifting. I suppose if it were easy, my father and partner would have changed the company years ago. Or maybe they reached their goals, and where the company is now is where they thought they would be? Perhaps that's why my partner doesn't seem motivated to do things differently; possibly his goals have been reached, and maintaining the status quo is the result and ultimate achievement of his lifetime of professional effort. More questions that don't provide me with answers about my business, or my share of our business, I should say, and where I want things to go over the coming years.

I think the conversation later today with Julian needs to focus on where we want to go, not where people think we should go, not where society may tell us we should like to go, and not necessarily where we have been or are progressing towards. I need to focus on creating my vision. If I'm going to spend the remaining years of my life, or at least my professional working years, working, I should pursue something that makes me happy.

I moved from the lounge to the elevator area and pressed the down button. One of the four doors opened, and I entered to be whisked to the lobby. While waiting for my Uber under the covered drive, I felt a change in my perspective. The lobby's height offered a different view of the harbor than the view from the front of the hotel. The water is barely visible because of the street and grassy areas between the hotel and harbor; the condo building across the street now obscures my view of the harbor and sailboats; the cars whizzing down Lockwood Drive offer a distracting noise from the potential serenity of the area. *Perspective matters.*

The car pulled around, and the driver, leaning across the front seat to address me through the open passenger window, said, "Are you Sam? Headed to North Charleston?"

With a quick nod, I opened the door and entered the back seat. As I entered, I answered, "Yes, I'm Sam. How long is the ride?" The app said 22 minutes, but I wanted to be sure.

He responded, "With the traffic this morning, it should take us about twenty minutes; not too bad, considering."

"Ok, sounds good."

I never asked what "considering" meant and instead focused on the information for my upcoming meeting. I always do a better job reviewing the details of a situation before entering a meeting.

ACTION!

Don't drift with the currents of chance;
steer your career with purpose and resolve.

The uneventful ride left me standing in front of an industrial-looking, metal-sided building. Not much different from when I was selling industrial equipment. The only difference between then and now is the person I'm meeting and the product I'm selling. Ah, how much alike things are in the world of business; just another widget is all I'm peddling. Switching gears... I need to maintain a positive mindset. *It's all perspective.*

After making the pitch, having lunch with the client, and another Uber ride, I had some downtime in my hotel room to think about the conversation with

Julian. I reviewed the conversation repeatedly, mentally exploring each thought that occurred during and after the meeting. Perspective. Purpose. Objectives. Perspective. Purpose. Objectives. Vision. I think it all boils down to having a vision.

I need to consider what I want to accomplish in both my personal and professional life, not what anyone else believes I should achieve or strive for, but what I genuinely want to accomplish. My family life is wonderful, and I want that to continue; part of the entire concept of a happy family life involves having professional happiness. I need to feel fulfilled professionally so that I can give my family all that I can emotionally. They deserve that from me; they give that to me; they should get it in return.

I could give emotionally, even if I were unfulfilled professionally; I'm not sure they are mutually inclusive or exclusive. Good grief, wandering thoughts certainly are plentiful when trying to conceptualize a better life across multiple levels. I want to be happy in both my work and personal life; having a sense of contributing to my local community, society at large, and those I care about, including my partner, employees, wife, and children, is part of the holistic picture of who I am. It's essential to have balance across the board. It is more important to share a baseball game on a Thursday afternoon, not every week, but occasionally, than to be sure I work ninety hours every week. So, I'm right back to vision. Rome wasn't built in a day, and the home life is excellent; focus on the professional without excluding personal balance, and I should be good.

A text from Julian, *Walking in the lobby now.*

Response: *Meet you downstairs. In my room. There in less than 5 min.*

From my room, as I walked toward the elevators, I felt a blend of resolve and contentment. Recognizing the need for a more purposeful vision for my professional life lifted my spirits. The ride downstairs was smooth, and upon exiting the elevator, I noticed Julian sitting in a chair near one of the doors to the outside patio area adjacent to the pool. The view was inviting; as I approached Julian, he noticed me and stood up to greet me. I waved him off and gestured to stay seated. "No need to get up. Good to see you again." Shaking hands as I joined him in the sitting area, I said, "Let's enjoy the view here; you seem to have found a pleasant spot to continue our conversation."

Julian responded, "Yes. I rather like this part of the lobby. It is pleasant enough and close to the coffee bar; even if I don't want a cup right now, the aroma is enjoyable. I must admit, my mind has not been on coffee since this morning. Instead of coffee, I have been exclusively pondering my next steps."

Sensing he was eager to share, I tabled my thoughts for a moment. "Oh really? And what conclusion did you reach? I get the feeling you must have arrived at some decision based on your anxious manner. What's on your mind?"

"Quitting," he responded to my utter surprise.

"What?"

"Yes, quitting."

I was shocked. "Alright. Talk to me. What will you do if you quit? Tell me about what you're planning."

Since we started discussing work this morning, Julian smiled the first seemingly genuine smile. He said, "I'm not talking about quitting work or leaving the accounting profession. I'm talking about shifting the focus of my current business, while simultaneously entering the job market. After we met this morning, I had a few revelations about what I want to do with the rest of my professional life. First, I do not want to manage a company. I played out the various scenarios in my mind regarding growing, reshaping, and clients...you get the picture. I considered changing directions towards a more traditional type of firm. The idea seemed moderately appealing at first because it was comfortable. It is exactly the work I did when first entering the accounting profession. Consider that type of labor comparable to an old shoe. It fits comfortably, but I don't want to wear it to the dance."

I jumped in as he took a small breath. "I don't think I've seen you this excited about any aspect of anything you mentioned this morning. What made you think this way or, more accurately, what empowered you to think this way?"

He smiled in a way that conveyed some sense of purpose or overall relief from a burden. "I'm not sure if anything particular inspired me. Clarity just seemed to settle upon me as I imagined my life in twenty years. I want my family to be happy. Part of my family's happiness is my own happiness. A significant part of my happiness is that my work life provides a measure of fulfillment. None of those thoughts or wishes makes a complete picture; taken together, they helped me form a plan."

Amazed at his thought process and maybe even slightly envious, I said, "I am a little stunned; my thoughts have been along the same lines since this morning. I must admit, I'm still lacking in anything resembling the conviction you appear to have regarding your career direction. Perhaps you could share a little more about what you decided, and it might help me with my thoughts."

Julian began, "After we parted ways this morning, I went to my favorite park by the bay. The one with the magnificent houses that are big and colorful, you know, the ones in loads of pictures and featured on the carriage tours. Anyway, while there, I began thinking about what I want from life. Is it money? Is it power? Is it an easy lifestyle? I've always joked about buying a sailboat and sailing away to the Caribbean, yet I've never so much as taken a sailing lesson. It is merely idle thinking, an escape from the pressure of a week, a day, or a moment that is stressful. Sailing away on a boat is not my reality. I enjoy working when I feel that the work being performed is for the greater good of a company, its customers, or society. Figuring out how to structure a financing deal so a company can add a new facility, helping raise funds from investors, seeking political support to re-zone an adjacent property to allow expansion of a division, or adding another building to serve clients, or anything like that, is all fun and exciting to me. I have done excellent work in the past. I just got discouraged in my old role."

I leaned in and said, "During our earlier conversation, you mentioned waiting in line for your chance to advance within the leadership hierarchy. Is that the only reason you were discouraged? Not that the reason isn't strong enough. I'm just trying to understand your perspective better."

Julian, picking up on my increased interest, further elaborated on his newfound clarity. "That was part of it, but the dominant reason was something more. It occurred to me while contemplating the events as they transpired, meaning I examined them from my newfound perspective, and decided that my path was not blocked or my progress impeded by another person. My imagination inhibited my progression, meaning my ability to see beyond the surface elements of my position. This occurred to me as I sat in the park overlooking the bay. The little waves on the surface seem so small, almost calm at times, yet beneath the surface exists a powerful current. The bay area of Charleston is not a small boat type of area. Besides the ships and other assorted large boats traveling through or around the bay area, the currents are powerful. At least once every summer, some person ventures out in a small craft, doesn't pay attention to their navigation, and is swept into rough water; they either get a good scare or get into serious trouble. Either way, it's not what they expected."

He continued, "It occurred to me that my career was similar. Like the bay currents, beneath the surface of my career, things moved swiftly as it pertained to time and opportunities. Much like the person who doesn't pay attention to their navigation on the bay, I ignored the currents; looking back, I could have seized several chances to direct my career in a more enjoyable and satisfying direction. This morning, I realized some folks are happy to let the wind and currents take them where they may; luck and hope are the plan. That doesn't work for me. I need to steer my career and life in the direction that works for me. That said, I've decided I need a new job. Not just any job, I already have one of those. I need to find a place where the value of what I can bring to a company will be appreciated."

I understood his thought process and stated, "When you spoke of quitting, what you meant was not to just quit doing the type of work you are doing, you are talking about quitting on the idea of having your firm. What will you do?"

"What I've already done, not what I will do," Julian declared, a hint of triumph in his voice. Once I had a plan, I consulted with my wife. After confirming her support and approval, I called an executive recruiter and tossed my proverbial hat in the ring. I told her what I'm looking for, and she is already working on finding a good fit. Specifically, I am seeking a second-in-command position where the person in charge will mentor me for a leadership role in a division or the firm within a few years. It seems so obvious to me now; it is a little surprising I didn't see it before."

Julian continued, "I emailed my old boss and asked for a meeting tomorrow morning. Assuring him I have no plans to return to work, the purpose of the meeting is to share my ideas for my future; he has already agreed to meet. The most important thing is that I need his help in getting a new position. He may attempt to get me to return, but that's not what I want; if I were to return, I would feel those same old feelings of frustration. I need a fresh start, one that doesn't entail moving backward. My heart wasn't in the venture of opening my shop. My passion is in building a manufacturing facility or expanding facilities to help the members of a community."

A little stunned at how quickly Julian arrived at this large of a decision and acted upon his thoughts, I said, "Wow. That is a lot to absorb. I'm surprised at how quickly you acted. In the space of a few hours, you decided on a path and took action. I'm impressed, and if we're still being transparent, a little frustrated at my inability to progress beyond the first steps of solving the challenges associated with moving forward personally and professionally. My thoughts began in a similar place, with a desire to be happy, provide for my family, and find fulfillment in my career. I made little progress beyond that point, but your comments may help me."

The conversation turned towards family for a few moments, and realizing my time was nearly at an end for the visit, I said, "Julian, I hope we can do a better job of keeping in touch. I'm thrilled for you regarding your fresh path and keenly interested in how things progress over the coming weeks. Let's exchange emails or calls as we make progress. It would be helpful to hear about your successes and how you handle unforeseen setbacks. I want to share the same if that's ok with you?"

Julian responded in the affirmative, and we bid each other farewell. As I made my way towards the cab and ride-app area for the trip to the airport, I couldn't help but feel uplifted at how Julian had progressed towards building a better future professionally in such a rapid way. Granted, a new job may take a few weeks to secure; I have no doubt news of Julian's success will come via email or phone soon. I have some work to do if I plan to deliver news of progress in the coming weeks and months.

MORE THAN COFFEE

*The difference between a business and
a hobby is that one makes money
and the other takes money.*

The local coffee shop, striving against the well-funded chains, is often the dream of a fellow coffee lover. The more I travel, the more I notice that one or two brands are replacing local shops; this seems especially true in larger towns and cities. When I was working on my MBA, I chose a Global Business Project instead of a thesis. That choice meant a trip to London. It was an experience I'll never forget. One thing I noticed while in London was that two or three competing coffee shops dominated many corners. It seemed rare to see only one shop on a corner by itself.

A virtual coffee war has been brewing for many years. In America, the dominant player appears to be losing a minimal market share to competitors.

Now and then, an independent establishment appears to pop up and attempt to compete; the closest coffee shop to home is just such an example. No matter where I go these days, I seem to think more about how well or poorly a business is being managed. Perhaps this is because I'm thinking more about how my business could improve. Regardless, the coffee shop seems to be a perfect example of how to invest money and lose it all because of poor business decisions. Perhaps my local shop will be the exception and last more than a year or two, becoming more than just a dream for a coffee lover. Regardless, I expect my visit to be enjoyable.

The coffee is excellent; perhaps that's why I keep coming back. Or maybe it's the plush sofas and chairs in the corner? Perhaps the thought of driving two miles from home to enjoy a few moments reading my news feed while enjoying a good cappuccino feels too much of a stretch for the luxury of excellent coffee. Maybe the espresso maker in the office should be used more often. No, this is better. Indulge the senses and awaken the mind for less than five dollars. It's a cheap habit, and one I plan to keep.

Upon settling into one of the comfortable, deep brown leather chairs in the cozy back corner of the shop, I opened my iPad to read today's business articles. I occasionally glanced around, taking in the sights of new customers walking in, enjoying the smells of coffee being ground, and sipping a little of my favorite beverage. During one such glance, I noticed some employees looking my way while mildly gesturing towards the front door. It seemed a little strange, and I wondered what the topic of discussion in the little huddle might be; the mystery seemed about to be solved as one server started walking in my direction.

The barista said, "Hi Sam, it's good to see you. I was in the back when you came in. Enjoying your usual?"

I replied in the affirmative, "Enjoying a brief break before a meeting. I love coming in here to get my mind prepped for the upcoming day. How are things with you?"

She countered, "Things are great, except for a minor mistake I made this morning. That's why I came over to chat for a minute. I was wondering if you might help me out with a small favor?" My questioning expression likely prompted her to continue with her request. "I neglected to put a *'Reserved'* sign in that back corner today. The owner hosts group meetings on Mondays and Wednesdays; he has members of his foreign language class come here to study. I'm embarrassed to ask, but could I trouble you to move to another spot in the shop? I'm sorry about asking and also about not putting up the sign earlier."

"Happy to move, no problem at all. Let me gather my things, and I'll move to the front corner table by the window." She thanked me again as she returned to the counter area to retrieve her '*Reserved*' sign. I moved to the window seat in a slightly less comfortable chair, as a little too much light was coming through the windows; the sun was at the perfect angle to interfere with my reading. Naturally, I started thinking about this business and what I had just learned about priorities and customer service.

My first thought was that the owner appears to have a hobby rather than a business. Asking a paying customer to move from a preferred to an alternate seat seems a little absurd. It wasn't so much the inconvenience of moving that bothered me as much as the thought of how fundamentally wrong it seemed that a business owner would put their needs ahead of the customer. What other things were happening that I didn't see? I thought about other comparable, equally flawed situations. It's akin to a renowned chef reserving the best table to have a casual fast-food meal with her friends on a Friday evening.

Okay, maybe that's a bit too extreme as an example, but the unease was still present. The seat was indeed a little less comfortable, and the lighting was slightly intrusive and annoying. I glanced about and pondered my new perspective; people seemed happy and chatting just the same as before. The smells and sounds were the same, but something was missing. The charm seemed to have lost a little luster for my tastes.

Was this shop a business or a hobby? *The difference between a business and a hobby is that one makes money and the other takes money.* Which category did the coffee shop fall into? My guess is a hobby. That forced me to think beyond my customer experience and ponder the experience my business provided. What details had I overlooked that might affect a client's experience or influence a decision to remain a client?

As I considered some recent client interactions, the owner's group gathered in the corner. They seemed happy, chatting with each other in a friendly way. They seemed a little different from the rest of the customers; most seemed to hover over their coffee and, if chatting with someone, appeared a little more subdued. Maybe the owner was happy with the blend of the two atmospheres; perhaps the owner didn't notice. I wonder what not noticing might cost the shop in business.

Every business is distinctive, even coffee shops. Not every person wants to enjoy the same coffee experience; that was evident years ago in London. What may be enjoyable for one person doesn't work for another in the slightest. Maybe my minor annoyance at moving seats wouldn't bother most people; perhaps, my journey of business evaluation was a little too deep, too critical, for the everyday business. Was I looking for something or seeing something that wasn't there? Maybe. Every company must strike a balance between copying a competitor and creating a unique customer experience.

As I finished my coffee and packed up my iPad, I made a mental note to pay closer attention to how my business treated its customers. There was always room for improvement; however minor, this experience served as a valuable reminder.

I cast a glance back at the shop as I exited. This shop might be capable of more than just making it; Perhaps it would thrive because it was a viable alternative to the big brands. It could also become another loss resulting from flawed business strategies born from poor customer service. In any case, I planned to come back for the great coffee and a chance to think over these everyday business lessons.

Stepping into the fresh morning air, I felt a renewed sense of purpose. Today provided another excellent opportunity for me to evaluate every level of customer interaction. What started in the coffee shop, I'd continue in my office. From my employees to clients on the phone, every experience needed to add value. After all, *the little things often make the most significant difference.*

WHERE FOOD MEETS PURPOSE

Great businesses don't guess; they plan
every detail with purpose and vision.

It was another one of those nights at Rochelle's, the kind where the place feels like home even though you're technically a guest. My wife and I were regulars; we probably visited at least once a week, although sometimes life got in the way and it was closer to every other week. No complaints, though. It was the spot where you felt like part of the family the minute you walked in. Rochelle had a unique way of making everyone feel welcome. The décor felt warm and inviting, and many of the staff members knew regulars by name, drink preferences, and minor facts about their lives. The vibe was casual, yet purposeful. This warmth created an amazingly positive overall experience.

When we arrived, we were greeted by the usual bustle: plates clinking, servers darting in and out of the kitchen, the hum of laughter and conversation swirling around. This wasn't a fine-dining kind of place, but you wouldn't mistake it for anything less than special. You could tell from the minute you sat down that Rochelle wasn't just running a restaurant; she was curating an experience every night. And it wasn't just about the food either. She was always thinking ahead, always figuring out ways to elevate the dining experience without making it feel like she was trying too hard.

Tonight, she had something new to show us.

Rochelle walked over to our table, that familiar, easy smile on her face. "Sam, Grace, it's good to see you guys. Would you mind if I sat and shared a few minutes?" Grace and I nodded in the affirmative, and Rochelle pulled out the chair across from us and sat down, leaning in like we were about to share secrets.

"Is everything good tonight?" Rochelle glanced about, scanning our table like she was mentally checking things off her list. A quick motion toward a server had him move in our direction to offer some warm rolls fresh from the kitchen and serve a couple of waters.

"We're happy to be here, as usual. Grace and I were commenting on the special menu selections. This new lamb thing you've got going is enticing. We love the variety."

Rochelle grinned, clearly pleased but not surprised. "I'm glad you like it. I've been working with a local ranch for a few months to source some top-quality lamb. We've been experimenting with various ways to showcase it; we've been working to deliver burgers, chops, and more. You might start seeing some of those as Saturday specials. The ranch is small, but they're doing incredible things, and I want to bring that quality to the table."

Grace leaned forward, her interest piqued. "Lamb burgers? That sounds amazing."

"It's not just about throwing something new on the menu," Rochelle explained, her tone thoughtful. "It's about ensuring it fits with what people already love here. The lamb will bring a different energy to the menu, but it'll still feel familiar, something everyone can get into."

We were already sold. Rochelle had this uncanny ability to know exactly what we'd enjoy before we even realized we were craving it. That's what made coming back so easy; there was always a surprise waiting for us, but never one that felt like it came out of nowhere. It always fits.

As she discussed the lamb partnership, I recalled her mentioning a trip to Italy the previous year. It was hard to forget, given how she had animatedly described her visit to a vineyard while sipping red wine with a group of locals, deep in the heart of Tuscany. The trip had been more than just a vacation; it was a strategic move.

"Speaking of new ventures," Rochelle transitioned, "I've completed a deal for a small stake in an Italian vineyard and winery. Small place, but they've got some of the best reds I've ever tasted." She grinned, obviously proud of herself. "It's part of what we're doing with the lamb specials. The pairing's unreal, and I've got a great deal on some of their older vintages. It just felt like the right move."

"You're always thinking ahead, aren't you?" Grace offered a warm smile. Rochelle's reputation for strategic thinking had preceded her. It wasn't just about serving a sumptuous meal; it was about creating an experience that would keep people coming back.

"I'm always thinking about the next step." Rochelle seemed contemplative for a moment. "Not just in terms of the food, but in how we keep the whole dining experience fresh and exciting. My customers deserve it."

That's when I realized what made Rochelle's place so special. It wasn't just the food, though the food was undeniably incredible. It was the way she thought about her customers, how every decision was made with them in mind. She wasn't trying to break the bank or push the boundaries of fine dining. It was about delivering high-quality, excellent meals at an affordable price.

"We try to keep things real, you know?" Rochelle added. "This is a neighborhood spot. It's not about impressing people with fancy stuff. It's about creating the kind of place where people want to come back to, where they know they're going to have a meal that blows them away every time, but at a price that makes sense."

We were nodding along in agreement. That's why we kept coming back. Every visit felt personal, like Rochelle was taking the time to think about our experience, not just the meal itself. Whether it was the menu curation, the new partnerships she was forging, or how she empowered her staff to make every diner feel special, this was about more than just the food. It was about the culture she had built here. The service.

The little touches. The sense of community that went beyond just eating and drinking.

"So," looking at Grace, "what do you think? Should we give the lamb a shot this weekend?"

She raised an eyebrow. "Oh, I'm all in. I can already taste those burgers."

Rochelle stood to leave, but not before one last glance at the table. "I'll send over a sample of one of my favorite reds for both of you to try. Have a wonderful dinner and let me know if you need anything."

With that, she was off, moving through the restaurant like the conductor of a symphony, every element in harmony, always thinking a few steps ahead. And that's what made Rochelle's restaurant not just another place to eat. It was a place where you knew you would be surprised, delighted, and treated like family.

Rochelle possessed vision, purpose, and efficiency. Purposefully, she developed a plan for success. Every decision she made regarding her restaurant and customers had a rational purpose. She made excellent choices with the lamb and wine. Wow, that's impressive!

BEYOND THE BIKE

Business isn't just about profit; it's about lifting people, teaching values, and building something that lasts beyond the bottom line.

A blue-sky Saturday morning's gentle warmth promised a sunny day to follow. Summer is fantastic. My mood was exceptionally positive, and I had some free time before heading to the local hardware store to pick up a few items. Loving to mix a little business with personal time, I planned to stop by Billy's business, *Chilly Willy's AC Service*. Billy was an old friend of my father's and had been handling the service of our family's appliances and air-conditioning units for years. He was also one of our clients; his company was among the first to purchase insurance from my father when he established his business.

My father really liked Billy; he wasn't just some guy who fixed things, he had a knack for always making you feel like any problem could be solved. The issues may or may not be related to appliances or air conditioning units. Billy was a life problem solver; it appeared on the outside like he approached every interaction to either enhance someone's experience, impart a life lesson, or otherwise relieve a burden. When he interacted with you as a customer or client, his attention seemed laser-focused, like you were the only person in the world he wanted to pay attention to at that moment. It was the epitome of being present in the moment that seemed to attract people into his orbit.

My wife told me that Billy was hosting a yard sale, so maybe Billy was mixing a little business with personal time. There was only one way to find out: to visit.

When I arrived at Billy's shop, I noticed activity at the house next door. Knowing this was Billy's home, I assumed Billy was probably hosting the yard sale at his house and not his business. Already pulling into the shop parking lot, I noticed Billy standing near the front door. As I approached him, I saw a little smile on his face, which seemed to show self-satisfaction or the enjoyment of a moment.

Getting out of the car, I said, "Hi, Billy. How's the day going?" He nodded toward the customers gathered around some appliances and air-conditioning units in his driveway and said, "Things are looking great today. Little Billy is over there taking care of people and moving some inventory. Overall, based on how many sales he has made, I'd say today is shaping up to be way better than average."

Looking a little more closely at the row of items for sale, I said, "It looks like the entire driveway is filled with refrigerators, air conditioners, stoves, and dishwashers. Is it a yard sale or an appliance sale? Wouldn't it be better if it were in your shop?"

He nodded and smiled. "Sure, I could hold the sale in my shop. As a rule, I only sell new merchandise in the showroom. All the stuff over there is from a side project named '*A Bike for Little Billy*'."

I chuckled while thinking, here comes a life lesson imparted by Billy. My detour was already turning out way better than expected. I gestured towards Little Billy and said, "Ok, Billy, you have my attention as usual. I'm waiting for the lesson; you always seem good for one. If I'm being transparent, I didn't just stop by to see you today because you're one of our company's most long-standing clients; I'm visiting business owners we have relationships with and seeking to gain some wisdom or life lessons. Without digging around for it today, you seem to have one ready to serve up on a silver platter. I'm all ears."

Billy's demeanor emanated pride as he said, "Little Billy approached me about two months ago and asked me to buy him an electric bike. Many of the kids he spends time with at school have an electric scooter or bike, and he wants a bike. I asked him how much a bike cost, and when he told me, I was shocked. I searched online and realized he was correct; the average bike costs about $1,800. I told him I would think about it. Perhaps it would make a great Christmas present or birthday gift. An idea struck me as I wrapped up the day at work and walked over to the house—a life lesson coaching opportunity. I'm always looking for those types of moments and should have thought about it right away. I suppose the sticker shock of the bike price delayed my thoughts a little."

Billy smothered a chuckle. "As I walked in the door and hugged my wife, she said, What's got you smiling like the cat that caught the canary? I replied that Little Billy had just given me a grand opportunity to teach him about the very adult values of opportunity and worth."

"So, Sam, I'll share it with you just like I shared it with Judy. Little Billy wanted something that had a pretty surprising price tag. The bike cost would mean nothing if I could leverage it into a life lesson about the value of money and the time to earn it. If Little Billy learned a little about sales along the way, then so much the better. It occurred to me I could have him help me in the shop for an hour or so a day during the week and a few hours a day on Saturdays. Instead of paying him to do menial tasks, I would have him shadow my every decision related to repairing some used appliances. People give them to me all the time to haul away, when it costs more to repair than buying a new unit. Normally, I sell them online for people to use as parts. If Little Billy could learn about the appliances, he might gain enough knowledge to talk about them to other people. If he could talk about them and was sufficiently motivated, he might learn to sell them."

I immediately saw where this was going and gestured towards Little Billy, who was interacting with people three or four times his mature age of ten. I said, "I'm assuming that all of this is the product of some deal you made with Little Billy and a couple of months' worth of repairs?"

Billy nodded and said, "Yes sir, that is correct. I told my boy, if you want that bike, you have to earn it. I proposed taking a couple of months to work with me, learn about the appliances, and then host a yard sale. I told him that since the appliances were free, the business deal we would make would be that we take the sales price, subtract whatever we spent on parts and yard sale ads, and split the profits 50/50. I won't tell him, but Judy and I will put the 50% we get into a college fund. Win, win all the way around."

I overheard conversations between Little Billy and customers as Billy and I walked across the parking lot towards the yard sale. I observed Little Billy approaching a customer. He asked about the person's needs and wants, then suggested a window air conditioner. It wasn't easy to accept that he was just ten. I thought and said to Billy, "I believe the kid is a natural!"

Billy beamed with pride. "As of about 9:30 this morning, Little Billy is halfway to his bike. That sense of accomplishment of taking something from the point of not working to being repaired and now to being sold means a lot, and so will that bike when he gets it. He will know he earned it through his hard work; his mother and I will know he honed some important life skills. It's a beautiful day."

"Billy, I agree with everything you're sharing. I think your son is way ahead of the curve. I know you could have easily bought the bike a few months ago, but this seems like a much better course of action. I think Little Billy is getting a brilliant head start on life. If he keeps selling like that, I may want him to come work for me!"

Billy laughed and said, "I saw him first. I have dibs."

The more I watched, the more I realized how much Billy had put into building not just his business, but a culture of work and responsibility. Recalling past interactions between Billy and my father, other customers, or Billy's staff, strengthened some of my earlier impressions of Billy. I felt more strongly than before that Billy was constantly engaging in a way for the betterment of the person he was interacting with during any exchange. It wasn't just about fixing appliances or refurbishing pre-owned units; it was about teaching his son the value of hard work and persistence. It was about helping a community member or employee through a hand up, not a handout. And in that, he was teaching us a little about how to treat those around us.

Reaching out my hand to give Billy's a shake, "Billy, I'm going to take off. Thanks for sharing a few minutes of your time. This visit was more inspirational than you know."

"Great to see you, Sam. Thanks for stopping by for a visit. If you ever need anything, let me know. I'm always happy to help."

As I pulled away, I kept thinking about the experience. It resonated with me on many levels. Not only was Billy helping his son, but he was also selling appliances at heavily discounted prices to community members.

I thought about a book I had been reading a little each morning that referenced a couple of companies and how the leaders of those companies held the company's values in the highest regard—according to what was shared in the book, WD-40 and The Container Store both exemplified lifting employees, serving the community at large, providing unmatched customer interactions, and building something that would last beyond the people who built the companies. In contrast to typical business school case studies, those stories introduced the concept of Conscious Capitalism, moving beyond conventional business and capitalism. Profit is not the only motivator; instead, it results from caring for both internal and external customers, strongly signaling to all involved that the company's objective is to serve as many people as possible exceptionally and to grow and thrive forever.

Wow! I just saw that in action. The business is half the size of mine, yet I'm sure that's what I witnessed. Small or large, creating a culture of purpose that matched what would give me the highest level of self-identified success seemed more possible than ever.

A STEP TOWARD THE THRONE

*Start small. Build understanding.
Bridge vision to action.*

The day was already off to a promising start. Our civic group breakfast had been full of energy and a real sense of purpose. Our new project offered five scholarships of $2,000 each to students attending a trade school or university. It wasn't a big program yet, but it felt like a meaningful step; something tangible we could accomplish together.

As the meeting adjourned and people dispersed, I observed a quiet strength displayed by people I hadn't previously viewed as heroic. Unsung heroes, such as my wife, who made many sacrifices that went unnoticed, or Billy, who believed that businesses should have a positive social impact beyond just profit. Our group contained many who reminded me that unless you look closely, it is challenging to spot all the heroes in a community. It was inspiring.

Those moments planted the first seeds of something bigger; something I was starting to understand. Maybe this was my chance to move beyond simply running a business and become the leader who actually changes lives.

Pulling into my office parking lot, I was eager to tackle the workday. Grabbing my coffee and bag, I walked toward the front door. My spirits were high; for some unknown reason, it seemed like the perfect day to solve some challenges.

Headed to my desk, I walked past the front reception area, saying hello to all. Bright smiles and positive attitudes were prevalent; no challenges there. My problems were bigger than our current team. Maybe this was the day to aim toward something significant.

I settled into my office chair, the leather still stiff from years of use, and pulled out the notebook I had used earlier on the plane after meeting Paul and Gennie at the airport in Charlotte. The cover was plain;

the edges worn from hurried scribbles and constant flipping, but inside it held the promise of something more: a system I hoped would bring clarity to the questions of my business. In big letters, underlined at the top of the page, was Throne of Profit System; under that, at the top of three columns, were ToP Strategy Model, ToP Action Model, and ToP Measurement Model.

An unusual quiet pervaded the office. The indistinct murmur of voices, the occasional ring of a phone, and the faint shuffle of footsteps created an almost meditative rhythm. Early morning sunlight streamed through the Venetian blinds, creating striped patterns on the floor. I glanced toward the front office, where Julie and Marcus, two of my top employees, were engrossed in their morning tasks.

Those small moments revealed my first insight of the day.

Carrying some marketing materials, Julie walked from the counter to the copier. Marcus soon followed, balancing a coffee in one hand and a file folder in the other. Each made the same journey, back and forth, weaving through the cramped space between the front counter and the filing cabinet that stood stubbornly in the middle of the room.

My eyebrows drew together. Every trip seemed insignificant, but when multiplied over days, weeks, and months, it added up. Lost minutes, wasted energy, subtle frustration building under the surface. The issue was more significant than a simple inconvenience; it dragged on morale, efficiency, and even the customer experience.

I glanced down at my notebook and found the section titled ToP Strategy Model. The familiar triad stared back at me: Analysis, Vision, Goals. The words were simple, yet each was meaningful. I thought back on my chat with Jimmy at the golf course. Had I genuinely made any progress in comprehending my business? I worked through daily problems, made some decisions, and put in some effort here and there. But analysis? Genuine, thoughtful analysis? Honestly, that would be a no.

While reviewing the Analysis bullet points: Resources, Market, Delivery, I discovered the copier's role in the bigger picture. Its present position wasn't only inefficient; it was symptomatic of a business that had grown without deliberate planning.

Turning to Vision, I read the words Differentiation, Efficiency, and Alignment, and winced. Efficiency, I understood, and that was where the copier move fit. How about differentiation, then? What made my business unique? In terms of alignment, did my team understand the company's aims? Somewhere, I read about a distinction between internal and external customers. It's my responsibility to take care of Marcus and Julie, to make the business a place where people love to work and feel good about their day. Yet it's equally important to enhance their efficiency, however minor the impact.

Countless meetings and training sessions flooded back into my memory. My unclear goals were often lost in the details. My staff consistently demonstrated teamwork, collaboration, and positive attitudes. Despite their hard work and excellent performance, I questioned whether they fully understood my vision. Was my vision clear enough to me, to them? No one had ever asked about moving the copier or filing cabinets. Discussions about improving our efficiency were infrequent at best. It seemed like everyone was content with the way things were. That being said, the few requests didn't invalidate its potential or positive reception.

I flipped through the pages, scanning Goals: Immediate, Short Term, and Long Term, and considered the significance of each. Immediate wins, such as relocating the copier, could give momentum, but the bigger goals required more than quick fixes.

I exhaled slowly and jotted down a note in the margin of my notebook: *Start small, build understanding, bridge vision to action.*

I tapped the pen against the page as my thoughts shifted to the ToP Action Model: Purpose, Strength, Get it Right. My purpose was clear: to increase efficiency and make the business work better for everyone. Strength lay in my team's dedication. But "Get it Right" was trickier. It wasn't about moving furniture; it was about processes, tools, and time management.

The old filing cabinet, a stubborn, bulky obstruction, blocked the path. Nobody questioned its presence, yet everyone navigated around it. Moving it would be more than physical labor; it would be a symbolic shift.

Spontaneously, I reserved the upcoming Saturday morning on my calendar. This minor act was empowering.

The weekend was bright and warm when I hauled the filing cabinet out of the front counter area, muscles straining but spirit buoyed. Marcus teased me about turning into a furniture mover, but I didn't mind. The physical effort was grounding. I repositioned the copier where the cabinet had stood and stacked the files neatly into the back office. As I stepped back and wiped sweat from my brow, I imagined the ripple effect: less walking for my team, smoother workflows, happier customers.

Monday morning brought quiet validation. Watching Julie breeze between the front desk and the copier with fewer steps, and Marcus's surprised smile, gave me a quiet thrill. It wasn't a grand change, but it was a win, a measurable one.

I pulled out my notebook again and sketched a quick table under the ToP Measurement Model heading: Segment, Trends, Wins. I segmented my observations into employee movements and customer wait times. The trends showed increased efficiency, and the wins, Julie's lighter workload and Marcus's fewer trips, were real.

The notes felt more real now, more than just abstract ideas. They were tools. But as I moved into the following pages, the words and diagrams grew more complex. The ToP Strategy Model at Tier 2 details Vision as Differentiation, Efficiency, and Alignment. I understood efficiency, but what about differentiation? What was my business's edge?

I remembered Dad telling me repeatedly over the years: "Your competitors sell products; you sell trust." Could that be my differentiation? But how did I embed that into every action?

The alignment piece gnawed at me. Were my goals aligned with my team's? Did everyone understand the business's real purpose?

Flipping to the ToP Action Model, I read about Purpose not just as intention but engagement. Did my employees feel engaged? Did they see beyond daily tasks to the why behind the work?

Under Strength, I saw People, Capabilities, and Culture. I paused. I was proud of my team, but wondered if my culture fostered growth or just compliance.

The last section, Get it Right, outlined Tools, Processes, and Time Management. I realized that outside of moving the copier, I hadn't really optimized these. There was software I hadn't fully implemented, scheduling tools barely used, and processes that felt outdated.

Then came the ToP Measurement Model: Segment, Trends, Wins. Revenue lines, cost centers, margins, efficiency, velocity. The language seemed heavy, unfamiliar. My heart sank slightly. The framework, while powerful, was also complicated. Doubt began to creep in. Could I master this alone?

My eyes scanned the last notes, teasing with question marks under different terms. More details? What goes here? Did I write the right thing? Did Paul say something else here? What was Gennie talking about? She used an example, and I think I missed the point. There seemed to be so many dense thoughts with subcategories and interlocking concepts. This feels insurmountable. Or was it?

I closed the notebook, rubbing my temples. The simplicity of moving the copier was tangible and real. The rest, the deeper strategy and measurement, was a mountain I wasn't yet ready to climb. Or maybe I could, with some help. I scrolled through my contacts, found the one I wanted, and dialed.

"Hey Paul, it's Sam," I began, my voice steady but edged with a hint of frustration. "I've been working through the Throne of Profit System notes and workbook I downloaded. I applied the concept to relocate a copier in my office, resulting in increased efficiency. It was a win, seemingly a small one at first, but one that grew to be bigger than expected. After that, I attempted to tackle some larger challenges related to expansion, but the rest, including Tier 2 issues such as vision, culture, and measurement, remain unclear. I need help to break it down."

Paul's calm, familiar voice was a balm. "That's why it's a system, Sam. It challenges you, but it's meant to help you see things others miss. Let's set up a time. I'll help you cut through the noise."

I leaned back in my chair, the tension in my shoulders easing. This wasn't just a notebook now. It was a journey, one I wouldn't walk alone. I had a guide.

I looked again toward the office, the hum of my team energized by minor improvements and the promise of bigger change. The copier move was a start, a foothold. But the road ahead required more than effort; it needed clarity, partnership, and faith. For the first time, I was ready to truly sit on my Throne of Profit.

THE NOTEBOOK

Throne of Profit System™

ToP Strategy Model™

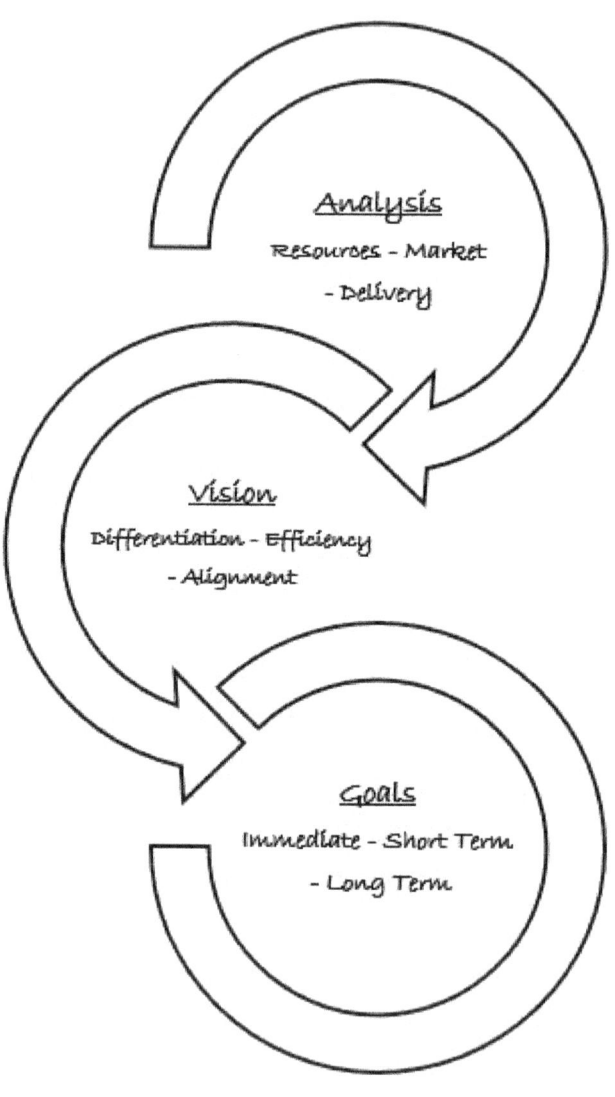

ToP Action Model™

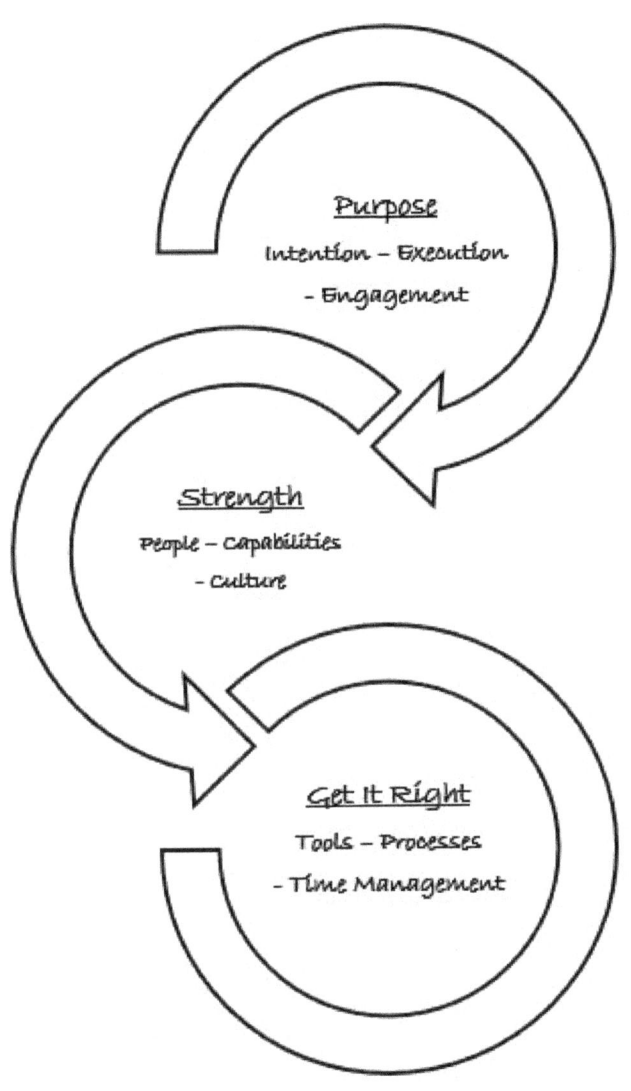

ToP Measurement Model™

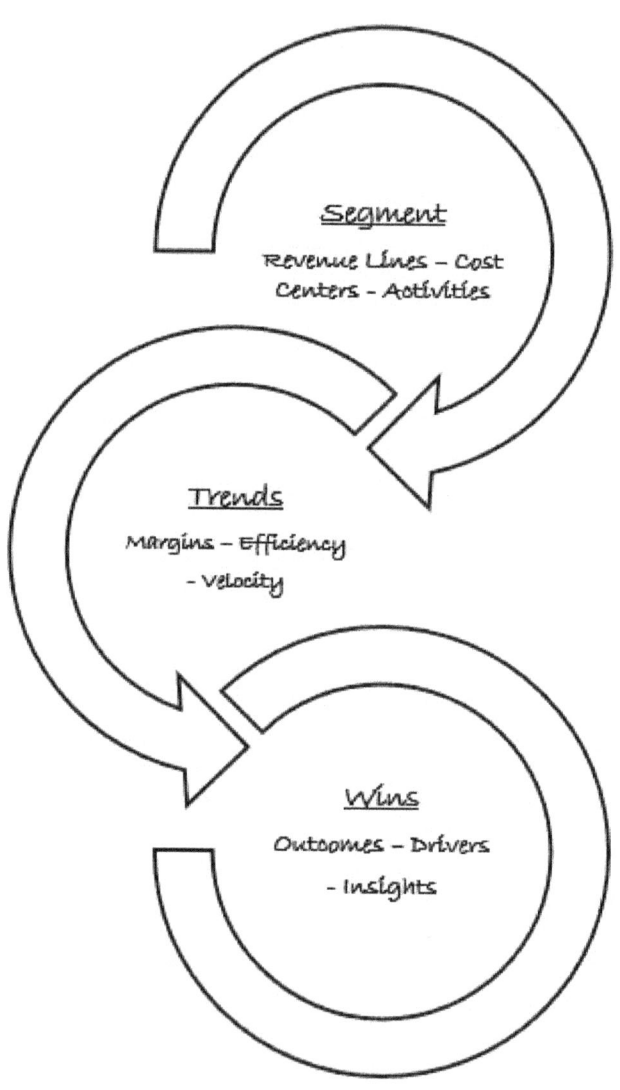

FINAL CALL — CLAIM YOUR THRONE

You've made it this far for a reason. You didn't pick up this book to be entertained. You picked it up to win. To stop guessing. To stop grinding in circles. To stop being the underpaid, overworked hero in a business that only works when you do.

Now you have the map.

The Throne of Profit isn't a metaphor. It's a position earned, not given; built on Strategy, Action, and Measurement. This book gave you the blueprint. The only question left is: Will you build?

Will you treat your business like the asset it's meant to be? Will you stop chasing tactics and start building a system? Will you claim your throne — or keep serving someone else's?

Because the throne will not wait forever.

If you're ready to act, turn the page. You'll find Author's Notes — a practical starting point, a strategic primer, the first step toward building your kingdom.

This isn't the end. It's your moment. Jump into some reflection time. Build your plan. Take the crown.

AUTHOR'S NOTES

MENTORSHIP OF STRANGERS

"The unexamined life is not worth living."
— Socrates

Chapter one starts where many of us have been: questioning our careers and if we're on the right path. The serendipitous meeting of Sam and Paul exemplifies a crucial life event that challenges our priorities and values. Paul's honesty, coupled with Sam's openness, uncovered underlying unhappiness, uncertainty, and a desire for more. People frequently ignore these moments in favor of distractions.

No matter what role you're in—running a business, working a job, or simply navigating life—this chapter raises one powerful question: *What happens when your path no longer leads where you thought it would?* Epiphanies and "eureka" moments aren't always how we resolve these types of issues. Such moments frequently happen while driving, during the quiet of early mornings, or even while waiting at an airport. This chapter encompasses more than just your current circumstances; it is about whether the path you're on is the one you want to keep following.

Pause for a moment; Settle your mind and thoughts. Let's take some time for self-reflection. The chapters were created to help shape your thoughts. If necessary, spend a few minutes reviewing the chapter. If the environment is too noisy or distracting, save the material for later. You could also do a draft now and revise it later. The objective is the same for each chapter. Think about any part of the chapter that spoke to you, prompted a thought about your business, or inspired you to examine some part of your business, position, or life a little more closely. Write down why that matters to you or is related to your situation. Save those notes. If you haven't done a self-reflection exercise before or it's been a while, here's the best advice I ever got for moments like this: *trust your gut. Don't overthink it—start writing.*

UNDERSTANDING WHERE YOU ARE RIGHT NOW

"If one does not know to which port one is sailing, no wind is favorable."
— Benjamin Franklin

Paul doesn't sugarcoat his opinion of business school. In his eyes, even the top programs fall short when it comes to addressing the real problems small business owners face. Sure, they can brag about ROI—big salaries, name-brand jobs—but that's not the same as running a business with your name on the door.

As Paul sees it, the gap between formal business education and real-world problem solving is vast, and most people don't even realize they're standing on the wrong side of it. Instead of encouraging Sam to go back to school or take a few weekend classes, Paul offers something more valuable: a shift in how to think. Especially in small businesses or tight-knit teams, solving problems isn't about textbook theory—it's about asking better questions and learning to think differently. You don't need a new credential. You need a new lens.

This chapter raises a broader question about the nature of education. Don't mistake Sam's path—or Paul's advice—as a universal map. Education comes in many forms. Some open doors. Some box you in.

Formal schooling isn't always the answer. You can see it in military veterans who crush it in the field but struggle in corporate roles. You can see it in dentists and doctors—excellent at their craft but overwhelmed by leadership, people management, or the business side. Being skilled in one lane doesn't mean you're ready for another.

That's why your growth path has to match your real needs. For some, that might be going back for a degree, and if that's your route, great. But for others, it might be mentorship, trade-specific leadership programs, certifications, peer networks, or just reading and applying what you learn.

There's no one-size-fits-all plan. There's only *your* plan. And it needs to fit where you are, where you want to go, and how you grow best.

SEEKING KNOWLEDGE

"The most difficult thing is the decision
to act, the rest is merely tenacity."
— Amelia Earhart

As the conversation continues in the next chapter, we witness a shift in Sam—frustration gives way to clarity. Sam, stuck in the grind of running a business without purpose or growth, listens closely as Paul reframes how strategy should really work. It's not about sticking to a rigid plan or clinging to what worked five years ago. It's about adapting in real time—staying tuned in to your customers while still moving toward your long-term goals.

Paul's approach challenges Sam to rethink everything: his assumptions, his processes, even his goals. What emerges is a powerful idea—success isn't just about working hard or staying busy. It's about being open. Open to learning, open to change, open to doing things differently than you have before.

You may hear this referred to as an "abundance mindset" or an "infinite mindset." Whatever the name, the principle is the same: those who keep their minds open—who stay curious, flexible, and future-focused, win more often than those who cling to what's always been.

We don't go deep into mindset in this chapter, but it's quietly running in the background of everything. Because in business—and in life—mindset usually trumps everything else.

If you need more knowledge, the right mindset will motivate you to seek it out. If you're facing challenges in marketing or operations, the right mindset will push you to ask questions, study, or get help. If the market shifts or the economy tightens, your mindset will determine whether you adjust or collapse. An open, growth-driven mindset beats the "we've always done it this way" mentality every time. And here's the best part: Even if you explore a new idea and come back to your original method, you'll have done it with clarity, not out of habit.

At worst, you confirm you're already on the right path. At best, you build something better. Either way, you move forward. And that's the point.

KNOWING WHAT TO MEASURE

"What gets measured gets improved."
— Peter Drucker

This chapter introduced you to The Throne of Profit System™. Building a business or managing a division isn't just about having a great idea or product to sell. You need a solid foundation like the three-legged stool. The three legs are *Strategy, Action*, and *Measurement*, which help launch an idea successfully and, more importantly, keep a business stable and growing.

The conversation between Paul, Gennie, and Sam used the analogy of a barstool to explain how one missing or shortened leg makes the stool unstable. This is precisely the way things operate in business. You can have the most excellent plan to launch a fantastic product, but if you never take action, nothing will happen. That "idea" that you had rolls around in your own echo-chamber for years until you see some other company delivering a similar product or service, or someone living a life you envy.

You don't need to be in that position. Analyze your idea. Decide if it is something you want to act on now, in the future, or never. Regardless of your decision, you can now focus on other tasks without any second-guessing. If the idea or project becomes actionable, this model promotes the next step… *Action.* Often overlooked, but vital. It's not about the first step; it is about all the steps. Although the first is usually the hardest or most challenging, thinking through the additional steps is also essential—finally, measurement. In a small business, or even in life, you need to measure success. Significant sweeping change rarely seems to happen. More often than not, the change one experiences is small and gradual. Failure to recognize that change is why most people revert to old ideas or concepts.

Many people look for the magical silver bullet instead of the minor or micro wins that signal the strategy was good and that you're now moving in the right direction. Think of it like the gym… people sign up in droves at the beginning of the year, go every day for an hour or two to walk, run, lift, work with a trainer, then at the end of a couple of weeks look in the mirror and don't see a total makeover, so they stop going. Weight loss and health aren't achieved as fast as an online download. Business decisions require some amount of time before you can tell if it was the right choice or plan. The only way to know is to track and measure.

In a small business, you can't afford to wait for quarterly reports or annual financials to make decisions. Instead, you should look at numbers in real time and search for those micro wins. Small wins add up and, over time, help you arrive in amazing places. 12-month, or even 365-day, rolling numbers should be examined as part of your P&L to see how your business is trending. If this isn't your strong area, don't worry; you're in good company. Find someone who is and get some help, or venture down a path of continual learning to improve. If you have to hire or contract a person to help, that's virtually always a better choice than the alternative of not understanding where you are in your business. After all, *if you don't know where you are, how can you figure out where you want to go and, more importantly, how to get there?*

ANALYZING YOUR BUSINESS FOR GROWTH

"The road to success is always under construction." — Lily Tomlin

In the chapter where Sam and Jimmy share a round of golf and engage in a frank conversation, the exchange has Jimmy lamenting the pressure of constant work and the lack of time to fully evaluate his business practices. During the discussion, they explore analyzing a business by examining financials, operations, and human capital. Jimmy's early journey—filled with wins and stumbles alike—offered a glimpse into the real experience of building something from scratch.

The chapter was primarily written hoping you might be reminded of some new venture or responsibility, and that memory or memories might inspire you to further reflection. This is another example of how continual learning is vital to business, especially small businesses.

You're encouraged to consider the importance of analysis in building a sustainable business. It isn't always enough to work hard; working smart and continually improving is vital in every business.

You must understand your resources, market, and how your business functions; this is critical for growth. Just like Jimmy had to take some time to reflect, I suggest you do the same.

Sources for a path of continual learning are in almost every market. Your local Chamber of Commerce may offer seminars or discussion groups. A local college or university may provide executive education courses or basic consulting services. Trade groups may offer certifications or training that will benefit you and your company for years to come. Franchise systems can be leveraged to create the ROI you want within a timeframe that makes sense to you. These opportunities allow you to meet more people and expand your support network. This list isn't exhaustive. If anything, it is barely getting started. Think about online sources, you can download workbooks, videos, and take courses... You get the picture. If you think something will help you learn, it's probably worth your time.

CHANGE BY DESIGN

"If you always do what you've always done,
you'll always get what you've always got."
— Henry Ford

Change, at its core, isn't about abandoning the foundation that brought you this far. It's about honoring that foundation by choosing to build something even more substantial on top of it. It means taking what worked—and what didn't—and using both as fuel for elevation. *Change requires intention, and intention demands leadership.*

Leadership isn't just about guiding others. It starts with guiding yourself, with stepping out of your habits long enough to see what's truly going on. Jimmy's moment of clarity can be summed up as, *I don't just want to work in the business anymore, I want to work on it*. It was a turning point. A shift from reaction to ownership. From surviving and reacting to strategizing and becoming proactive. Working on your business instead of always working in your business is a monumental step in taking your business to the next level.

This chapter calls on you to do just that... think more about working on your business.

There's a reason most people don't rise to the top of their industry: it doesn't happen by accident. Getting there—*and staying there*—requires strategy, discipline, and above all, self-awareness. That means you don't just notice what's going wrong—you investigate it. You don't just identify what's working— you study why. You stop coasting and start calibrating.

Begin with your market. Are you truly in tune with it? Do you know your competitors—not just by name, but by behavior, strategy, and positioning? How are they better? How are you better? How can you minimize their advantage or accentuate yours? More importantly, do you know your customers: their frustrations, their preferences, their unmet needs?

Recommit to analysis, not as a box to check but as a mindset. Take the pulse of your business with clear eyes. Don't flinch from the data. Don't justify away the flaws. Don't let momentum become an excuse to ignore what's changing beneath your feet.

Because change *is* hard.

Even when things aren't working, there's comfort in familiarity. The hesitation of many teams, companies, and leaders to adapt or improvise stems from this. We're powerfully drawn to what's familiar. If you find change difficult, it will be even more challenging for your team. That's when good communication is vital.

Bring your team with you.

Explain your reasoning fully, not defensively. Share the *why*, not just the *what*. Let people see your process so they can trust your direction. And once they see it, let them speak into it. Ownership doesn't come from being told what to do—it comes from being invited to help shape what's next.

Building a business, division, team, or culture requires intentional effort. It's a deliberate action. This design starts with you choosing excellence over convenience.

So, think about it for a few minutes... Where have you let things slip? What needs to change? Do you need to change? Change doesn't mean changing who you are or what the business is at its core...

change is about where you or the business can be improved.

Success isn't a matter of chance. It's the result of consistently choosing clarity over comfort, alignment over autopilot, and strategy over reaction. You can't fix what you won't face. But once you face it, you can finally build what you've always known was possible.

INVISIBLE EXCELLENCE

"People will forget what you said, people will forget what you did, but people will never forget how you made them feel."
— Maya Angelou

Few things are more universally understood—and widely dreaded—than a trip to the dentist. For some, it's routine. For others, it's anxiety-inducing. And for many, it's something to avoid altogether. That's precisely why it makes the perfect metaphor: in business, never assume your customer's experience matches your intention.

One of the most dangerous habits in business is assuming that, because a process is familiar to you, it must be easy for everyone else. Familiarity breeds blind spots. When you handle the same steps every day, it's easy to forget how they feel to someone new — or someone still uncertain. Your customer or teammate might be walking into your system feeling hesitant, overwhelmed, or unsure. Have you paused long enough to notice?

Just because it's efficient for you doesn't mean it's effective for them. The best systems are invisible to the user. The more intuitive, seamless, and human your experience feels, the more trust you earn. People shouldn't have to struggle through needlessly imposed structures or processes to get what they need.

And it's not just external customers. Internally, your colleagues are customers too. Departments rely on each other. Teams pass work hand-to-hand. Ask yourself: Are you delivering your part in a way that makes others' jobs easier, clearer, better?

Think back to the best dentist visit you've had — not because the procedure was pleasant, but because the environment made it tolerable. A clean, prepared, and calming space can reduce anxiety even when the work itself is uncomfortable. In business, it's the same. A well-managed experience doesn't remove the challenge, but it can completely transform how others perceive it.

So stop and step outside yourself. Walk through your business as a stranger. Strip away your assumptions and ask: "If I didn't know what I know—how would this feel?" *Because excellence isn't just about the outcome, it's about how people feel while they're getting there.*

Your business is more than a machine—it's a stage. Every touchpoint, every tone, every transition sends a message. And every message either builds confidence or builds tension. *Which are you creating? Don't just deliver the good or service.... Design it to be what it should be, an experience.*

EMBRACING PERSPECTIVE

"The best way to predict the future is to create it." — Peter Drucker

Some chapters don't just tell a story—they hold up a mirror. Ariel's chapter is one of those. What began as a simple conversation about opportunity turned into a masterclass in perspective. She didn't hand Sam a blueprint or a five-point plan. She offered something far more valuable: a new lens, one that provided an improved perspective.

How we interpret what happens to us—our internal narrative—shapes more of our lives than most people ever realize. And most of that narrative isn't original. It's inherited. We absorb patterns and beliefs from employers, mentors, families, and industries. We repeat phrases like "That's just how it is" or "People like us don't get to do things like that." What started as someone else's idea becomes our self-imposed ceiling. Remember... virtually all glass ceilings are self-imposed. Break out. Break through. Just break it.

That's really what this chapter is about: breaking that pattern.

Victim thinking doesn't always look like weakness. Sometimes it sounds logical, even responsible. But at its core, it's still fear dressed up as fact. Ariel's insight showed Sam what many people never realize: most of us are just one shift in perspective away from a breakthrough. She didn't just open the door; she revealed that Sam was the one holding it shut.

There'll always be those who prevent their own advancement. They will find excuses in timing, the economy, their past, or others' choices. However, the reality is: you're meant for more than a small life. To lead effectively, one must first confront and revise one's narratives with a clear purpose.

Shape your life into a heroic narrative by becoming the person you respect most, guided by self-awareness rather than pride. The optimal path benefits you, your family, your employees, your partners, and your community. The best version of you is found on this path, so pursue it.

Goal-setting gains importance at that point. Remember, at the most basic level; goals bridge your analysis of where you are in life or business to the vision of where you go or who you want to be.

Goals, however, are not created equal. Ambiguous plans don't qualify as goals; Genuine goals are specific, have deadlines, and align with your values. Overcoming these challenges, which will push you beyond your limits, is key to your success.

Simply put, you don't need an ideal background or perfect moment or situation. You need vision. You need to be brave. To grow into the person, you envision, you need discipline to act accordingly. Don't wait for the ideal moment. You're ready for a move. *The key is to decide that your past will not shape your future.*

So ask yourself: Where have you accepted limitations you should have challenged? What bold goals have you buried because they felt too inconvenient or too far away? This isn't about chasing busyness. It's about alignment—setting goals that matter, that stretch you, that remind you that you're still growing.

Ordinary people settle. Extraordinary people create a strategy and work towards making that strategy into their reality.

Every choice you make shapes the story you're becoming.

BEYOND THE BREAKAWAY

"It's not the load that breaks you down, it's the way you carry it." — Lena Horne

There's something quietly powerful about reconnecting with someone who once seemed invincible, only to realize they're navigating the same doubts, transitions, and internal questions you are. That was Julian. And that's why this chapter hits close to home for so many.

The truth is, uncertainty isn't rare—it's the rule. Especially for those bold enough to step away from safety and into something they believe in. Julian didn't just leave a corporate job—he walked away from a structure that rewarded predictability over possibility.

Like so many, he assumed that vision and hard work would be enough. But entrepreneurship doesn't hand out trophies for effort. It demands clarity, stamina, and adaptability. Sometimes, it's not a bold new chapter — it's a gritty, day-by-day test of endurance and self-belief.

And here's the part most people miss: Julian wasn't just building a business. He was rebuilding his sense of value.

Many people chase entrepreneurship to escape bureaucracy, burnout, or stagnation. But escape isn't the same as purpose. You can build a beautiful mission and still find yourself broke, frustrated, or uncertain whether you've made the right call. Julian launched a firm to help struggling businesses' noble and necessary cause — but in doing so, he realized a hard truth: passion without sustainability is a slow failure.

You can't pour from an empty cup. You can't help others if you're constantly on the edge yourself. This chapter isn't a critique — it's a caution and a call. A reminder that vision must be matched with strategy. Your purpose must be strong enough to carry you when the path ahead isn't clear.

Ask yourself: Is my job, business, or situation really aligned with who I am? Am I acting and living on purpose in my business, in my life? Am I only chasing the financial, or working towards something *more*? Have I settled?

You don't need to romanticize purpose, but you *do* need to define it. Because without it, you'll confuse busyness for progress. You'll make mistakes in the effort for effectiveness. And worse, you'll build something that doesn't feed your soul.

Numerous books and videos promote finding your purpose or discovering what truly drives you. If the answer doesn't immediately come to mind, or if you come up with a high number of objectives or goals, write down a list of things you want out of life or your business. Now, start crossing things off the list that are either redundant or that you would have or gain if you accomplish or achieve another milestone on your list. When you have something like 1-3 things left, stop and really reflect on what you see.

Don't worry about the things you crossed off the list --- Chances are, many of the things previously on the list aren't given up, so much as they will just come as a byproduct of you focusing on what really matters to you in a deep, meaningful way. When you build from that foundation, you create more than a business. You create alignment. And from that place, real momentum is possible.

You don't have to have it all figured out. But you do need to know why you're walking this road. Let your purpose be stronger than your fear. Stronger than your doubts. Because purpose, when truly owned, makes the struggle worth it.

FLEXIBILITY OVER FIXATION

"Everyone has a plan until they
get punched in the mouth." — Mike Tyson

Some chapters feel like a wake-up call. Others feel like a quiet mirror. This one does both.

Julian's story isn't the tale of a dramatic collapse—it's something more common, and in some ways, more unsettling: that slow, gnawing realization that your big idea might not work. Despite the vision, effort, and optimism, something still isn't clicking. The business hasn't broken, but it hasn't broken through either.

That's the nerve this chapter hits.

We often move through life with the unspoken belief that "Plan A" will work, because we *need* it to. Because it's what we told people we were doing. Because it's what our pride is attached to. But business doesn't bend to wishful thinking. The market doesn't respond to hope; it responds to value, execution, timing, and fit. Hope is not a business plan, a prospecting plan, a customer experience plan, or any other type of plan. Hope can inspire the beginning of something, of an idea, of a better life, of growth... but it cannot, should not, will not be the complete and total plan that works the best for all concerned. It is a catalyst, not the entire event.

Julian's pressure was real. Three months of credit left—a young family. A vision slipping into uncertainty. That's not theoretical—that's survival mode. But in that tension, something rare emerged: clarity. A forced honesty with himself. A willingness to look past sunk costs and reimagine what his business—and his life—*could* become. Julian's timeline was intentionally designed to be brief and prompt change.

This chapter isn't about glamorizing struggle. It's about extracting value from it. Most people don't hit a wall because they're lazy. They hit it because they're running hard in the wrong direction. Julian's pivot wasn't a defeat. It was a decision to align. To stop chasing what looked right and start building what *felt* right. To stop trying to rescue Plan A and begin creating something better, even if it starts with uncertainty.

Take note: sometimes, Plan A can be years in the making. The point is that you reflect and recognize the need to pivot from a person, situation, product, service, delivery model, tool, system, or even an entire business model, as Julian did.

If you're feeling stuck, stretched, or simply off-track, don't ignore it. Sit with it. Ask yourself: Am I plowing forward into something because I'm afraid of change? Am I holding onto something for the sake of hanging on, or am I actually committed to a purpose? What is really working? What isn't working? Be honest with yourself.

You don't need to throw everything away. But you do need to be willing to pivot.

Your Plan B might not be a downgrade; it might be the first time you're building from a place of self-awareness, not ego. Plan C might be your actual calling. Julian didn't quit because things got hard. He reinvented himself because he saw a better use of his gifts. That's not failure. That's leadership.

Whether you're navigating a crisis or just feeling misaligned, this is your invitation to ask more profound questions. To find the thread between your talent, your values, and what the market needs. And then to act purposefully and without needing every detail to be perfect first. Because sometimes, clarity doesn't come before the action. Sometimes it follows it.

If your vision no longer suits you, consider reshaping it. If your energy feels misplaced, redirect it. Success isn't about stubbornly sticking to the first version of your dream—it's about being humble and brave enough to evolve it. Don't wait for permission. Don't wait for disaster. Start moving. Start aligning. And trust that the right work, done in the right way, will bring the right momentum.

YOU MUST DO OR ELSE NOTHING IS DONE

"You don't have to see the whole staircase, just take the first step."
— Dr. Martin Luther King, Jr.

There's a quiet power in movement—a kind of inner ignition that separates those who wait from those who advance. For Julian, the turning point wasn't when everything was sure. It was when something felt *true enough* to pursue. This chapter wasn't about waiting for permission or perfection. It was about recognizing when the weight of inaction becomes heavier than the risk of taking a step forward.

Too many people get stuck on the threshold of a better life. They overthink, over-plan, and under-move. Others leap recklessly, chasing energy without direction. Julian modeled something different. He didn't move in haste or hesitation—he moved in alignment. He gathered what he knew, sought input or approval from the people who mattered, and then he acted.

That's the real art. Not acting blindly, but acting *intentionally.* Not chasing clarity, but trusting that it often arrives once momentum begins. Purpose isn't always loud. Sometimes it speaks in quiet confidence, the kind you can only hear once you start walking toward it.

This chapter was meant to wake something up inside you. To remind you that progress is rarely perfect, but it is consistently earned. You don't have to know the complete design of your future to take the next step. Many of the most successful people you admire didn't see the whole picture at the start. They saw just enough to know they were facing the right direction.

What matters isn't whether your plan is flawless. What matters is whether your actions are aligned with your values, with your strengths, and with the vision you're building. When all three converge, you begin to *get it right* more often than not. And each correct action builds credibility—with others, yes, but more importantly, with yourself.

Julian's story isn't about a monumental change. He didn't leave accounting work to run a bar in the Florida Keys. What it's about is choosing to pivot in a way that makes sense and truly meets the goals and purpose of a person or business. And that's the choice before every business owner, every leader, every person: Will you stay stuck in theory, or will you step forward in conviction?

So, here's the real takeaway: The Throne of Profit System is about forming a strategy, taking action, evaluating and measuring the outcome, and then refining that strategy, taking further action, and measuring again. Don't assume one plan, one action, and success begets all future success. Continual Improvement requires continual evaluation and the continuation of the cycle.

The throne doesn't wait for the perfect plan. It waits for the person willing to move toward it. Let this be your filter:

Act in alignment. Move with purpose. And let momentum do the rest.

INSIGHTS ALL AROUND US

"A satisfied customer is the best
business strategy of all."
— Michael LeBoeuf

    The coffee shop story could easily be dismissed as trivial; that would be a mistake. There are many business lessons available from Sam's short visit one morning to get a simple cup of coffee. The quick version is that Sam saw each step for what it was, something broken in the chain of customer experience. The forgotten sign, the move to a less desirable seat, and the owner being more focused on themselves instead of the customer experience... these things add up. None of them, taken alone, is the end of the world; collectively, they taint the experience. Think about it... when you pay $5 for coffee, it's clearly about much more than just getting a cup of coffee.

Small business owners often make a crucial mistake. They believe their job is to manage the operations. But the best don't just manage—they orchestrate experiences. They see every seat, every greeting, every subtle friction point as either a missed opportunity or a moment of magic. Sam became aware that most interactions provided such an opportunity to examine a process or an experience.

There's a dangerous line between a business that works for the owner and one that works for the customer. Many businesses lean inward, prioritizing convenience, routines, and personal preferences. But growth doesn't come from internal alignment alone—it comes from outward connection. The customer doesn't return because your systems make your life easier. They return because you've made *their* life better, even for just a few minutes.

This chapter is a quiet challenge. It asks you to look closely at your own business—at the way people are greeted, the way problems are solved, the way little irritations are ignored or handled. It asks you to consider whether your systems serve the experience or if they merely serve themselves.

Remember: you're not in the business of selling coffee, or homes, or dental services, or accounting services. You're in the business of creating moments that make people feel seen, understood, and respected. The coffee shop didn't lose a customer that day. But they may have lost something more subtle: a measure of trust—a thread of connection. And over time, that thread unravels.

The job, then, is to notice. To course-correct. To be the business that customers talk about—but for the right reasons. Not because the product was fine, but because the experience was unforgettable. That's what this moment was for Sam. And that's what it can be for you.

Let this be the lens: *It's not about the coffee. It's about how the coffee made them feel.*

LEAD, FOLLOW, OR GET RUN OVER

"Innovation distinguishes between a leader and a Follower." — Steve Jobs

Rochelle understood that delivering an exceptional customer experience didn't start at the front door. It began much earlier, with sourcing the lamb, selecting the wine, designing the room's flow, and training the team to care about the experience just as much as the menu. *It's what separates transactional businesses from transformational ones.*

It's about servers being careful when they clean a table, not to drop silverware; not only might it ding the floor or furniture, but it breaks the mood. The music and lights adjusted to the perfect levels depending on the time of day, silverware being rolled in the back somewhere versus by the register as you wait for takeout... little things matter.

That's the real lesson here. The food was great, but it was the experience-the process—that made it remarkable. It prompts a powerful question: What would it look like if you thought about your business the way Rochelle thought about her restaurant? Not just: *What do I sell?* But: *Where does it start? Who touches it along the way? What moments matter most? How do we deliver a great experience every single time?* This chapter invites you to think about your entire value chain—from raw input to refined outcome—and then assess the efficiency, emotional impact, and economic return of each stage.

Here's where the conversation turns from artistic to strategic. Because Rochelle didn't just rely on passion, she measured performance. ROI wasn't just a spreadsheet—it was the lived experience of her customers. She chose what to offer with care, tracked how it landed, and adjusted with precision. This is your invitation to do the same.

Start by imagining your product or service, not just at the moment of delivery, but from origin to outcome. Where can you make it better? It doesn't matter what you're delivering; think about every single person from suppliers to internal customers to the final recipient... how can you make each step along the way foster more trust, a better experience, and create efficiency for any person or entity involved... You get the picture. Be strategic about every aspect of the product, the service, and the delivery.

This means down to the smallest of items... Think of the "My Pleasure" at Chick-fil-A when you say thank you to an employee. It costs nothing, yet it creates efficiency throughout the system because employees know how to respond appropriately without having to search for a response that may or may not resonate or sound awkward. The customer can feel that connection at any location, regardless of geography.

And when it comes to numbers, don't use them like a report card you peek at every quarter. Use them like a compass. Segment your products. Tie the cost of goods sold directly to revenue streams. Watch trends — not just in gross sales, but in margins, feedback, repeat usage, and unit economics. That's how a business matures from guessing to guiding.

Many people wait for big wins to feel like they're making progress. But in reality, *business is often won by doing 1000 things 1% better, not by waiting and hoping that the one thing you get or do will make things 1000% better.*

So, take Rochelle's example as more than a story about a restaurant. It's a blueprint for how great businesses are run: Let this be your moment to refine your process. Revisit the customer journey. Then, get serious about measuring what matters because great companies don't happen by default. They happen by *design*. Just like a perfect meal—timed right, plated with care, and served with purpose.

Don't just deliver a product. Deliver an experience. Then measure whether it worked. That's how businesses rise.

PURPOSE DRIVEN LEADERSHIP

"Opportunity is missed by most people because it is dressed in overalls and looks like work." — Thomas Edison

The chapter about Billy and Little Billy is designed to remind you that not everything is related to a Profit and Loss statement; it was written to remind you never to forget some of the hopes and dreams you held dear in years past. Business can serve a higher purpose, and Billy exemplifies being in tune with the higher purpose of his company. To better the world around him, one person, one interaction, at a time.

Often, in business, when dealing with employees, it's easy to *buy the bike*, solve the problem, and make the sale. Billy opted for something more complicated and more lasting: He empowered his son to earn it. He taught Little Billy not just how to fix things or talk to customers but how to take ownership, believe in the value of work, and see the deeper purpose behind a transaction. That is a worthy goal and a powerful way to lead. It is also a fantastic way to inspire and develop future leaders.

This chapter aims to inspire reflection on your lasting impact. What inheritance awaits future owners, managers, and employees? How smoothly will the transition go? Will people remember you once you retire? Can the business continue without you? Only you can answer these crucial questions. The good news: it's still possible, even if you're just now reading this. *You are the author of your own legacy. What are you going to create?*

A STEP TOWARD THE THRONE

"You can build a business, or you can build a legacy." — Kiran Mazumdar-Shaw

In the final chapter, we follow Sam as he begins to translate the ideas behind the Throne of Profit System into tangible improvements inside his business. What starts as a simple copier move becomes a symbol of something much larger, a shift toward intentional leadership, strategic clarity, and operational efficiency.

Sam's story reminds us that often change or improvement can start small, but there is power in taking that first step. That is the reason Action is crucial. A score of people in the business world resign themselves to thinking of a great idea and never acting. Sam formed a *Strategy*, took *Action*, and *Measured* results. Win.

Using Sam's experience as a springboard, think about something small you can improve right now. Begin applying the ToP Strategy, Action, and Measurement Models—especially at the Tier 2 level (e.g., Efficiency, Culture, Time Management).

This section is not about solving everything at once. It's about building your first real foothold. One move, one win, one measurable shift. What "copier" is sitting in the way in your business? What small win can you claim today that gets you closer to your Throne of Profit? This will be your first small but powerful step.

Start small. Build understanding. Bridge vision to action.

EPILOGUE

This book is dedicated to all the small business owners who struggle with the questions every month, if not every week, like: How will I meet payroll this week? How can I pay my lease through the winter months? Will I ever make enough money to send my kids to college? Can I afford to pay my taxes? I need help; do I have enough money to hire help? I have an idea about getting more customers; should I do it? If so, how long? I wonder if I could get a loan to help expand my business? Would any lender ever give me a loan? Things are going great, and I want to turn my work from creating more work for me into building an actual business that serves others. I aim to create opportunities for individuals in my community who aspire to achieve more for themselves and their families. Serving the community at a higher level means I need more time and money to do that work. How can I make that dream come true? I want to save for retirement, but that seems so far from reality. How can I make that my reality?

Let me say to all the readers, I get it. Also, you're not alone. Every leader in business grapples with these same or very similar questions. The only difference between small business owners, division managers, or CEOs is the number of zeros they work with on their profit-and-loss statements. Not sure that's true… do a Google search for how many CEOs fail. Depending on the source, you'll likely find that approximately 40-70% fail, meaning they are fired, within 18 months. The Small Business Administration usually cites that around 80% of small businesses fail within 18 months and 50% within 5 years. The daily grind: payroll, debt, funding, facility changes, staffing adjustments, relocation, taxes… It's all part of leading and managing in the business world.

Remember, you don't have to make decisions. You can always get a job and collect a check from an employer if you want, but if you're going to lead a small business, a division, or a large business, you must lead. Leading doesn't mean making all decisions in a vacuum; use all available resources. This takes bravery and dedication. When you search for answers to perplexing questions, you don't always hear what you want to hear or get the answers you want. That is also part of being a leader, accepting the truth. Speaking of truth, here is some truth... Whenever you start to question if you made the right choice to keep going because times got tough or you don't like the current outcome of some decisions, remember, *"This is the business we've chosen."* Hey, what would a little discussion about business be without a quote from The Godfather?

You may not like that a pet project of your company or an investment you made in a division manager is precisely the wrong project or leader within your company. Your decision a year ago may have taken the company to the brink of failure. Imagine discovering that the best way to improve your consumer numbers is to push out advertising via a specific social media platform; hearing that, while simultaneously realizing you have no idea what that means beyond logging into Facebook to see what your kids or grandkids were up to that day, can be a tough pill to swallow.

Let success, not pride, be your focus. Use the tools and advice you have gleaned from all sources. Seek advice and inspiration, always. Raise others up, always. Be an inspiration to others and help fulfill their dreams. Take care of your community, be it the people working for you or those living around you. We're all in this together.

Capitalism is a good thing. It is not greedy to want freedom; freedom to take care of people around you, to help launch careers, foster relationships, inspire, teach, learn… these are all admirable things that improve the world. Trust yourself and surround yourself with people you trust. Values transcend balance sheets. Conscious Capitalism is the truest and most honest of dreams within a democratic society… Cherish the effort and the results.

THANK YOU AND GODSPEED

Thank you for reading *Throne of Profit*.
May your work be bold, your vision clear,
and your profit anchored in purpose.

For additional resources,
downloads,
or inquiries, please visit:
throneofprofit.com
or contact:
info@throneofprofit.com

ABOUT THE AUTHOR

William Hassell is a small business strategist, author, and the creator of the Throne of Profit System™. He developed the framework to help business owners lead with clarity, discipline, and measurable results across strategy, action, and performance.

He holds advanced degrees from Harvard and Cornell and has spent his career focused on helping entrepreneurs think strategically and build companies that are not only profitable but also worth leading.

Learn more at **ThroneOfProfit.com**

Intellectual Property and Use Notice

The Throne of Profit System™ is a proprietary business methodology created by William Hassell and owned by Throne of Profit, LLC. This system is designed to help small businesses clarify strategy, execute with discipline, and measure performance with precision.

The models, tools, and frameworks presented herein—including the ToP Strategy Model™, ToP Action Model™, and ToP Measurement Model™—are original works protected under United States copyright and common-law trademark law.

These materials may not be reproduced, distributed, adapted, taught, or used in derivative works without express written permission or a valid licensing agreement from Throne of Profit, LLC.

For licensing or certification opportunities, please visit throneofprofit.com or contact info@throneofprofit.com.

www.ingramcontent.com/pod-product-compliance
Lightning Source LLC
Chambersburg PA
CBHW040236110526
44582CB00021B/209/J